Policies that Perpetuate Inequality

Policies that Perpetuate Inequality

Colorblind Bias

Leland Ware

BLOOMSBURY ACADEMIC
NEW YORK • LONDON • OXFORD • NEW DELHI • SYDNEY

BLOOMSBURY ACADEMIC
Bloomsbury Publishing Inc, 1359 Broadway, 12th Floor, New York, NY 10018, USA
Bloomsbury Publishing Plc, 50 Bedford Square, London, WC1B 3DP, UK
Bloomsbury Publishing Ireland, 29 Earlsfort Terrace, Dublin 2, D02 AY28, Ireland

First published in the United States of America 2026

Library of Congress Cataloging-in-Publication Data
Names: Ware, Leland, 1948- author
Title: Policies that perpetuate inequality : colorblind bias / Leland Ware.
Description: New York : Bloomsbury Publishing, 2026. | Includes bibliographical references and index.
Identifiers: LCCN 2025034070 (print) | LCCN 2025034071 (ebook) | ISBN 9781666961874 hardback | ISBN 9781666961898 paperback | ISBN 9781978771598 epub | ISBN 9798216254492 pdf | ISBN 9798881897116 Subjects: LCSH: Race discrimination —Law and legislation —United States | Minorities —Legal status, laws, etc. —United States | Educational equalization —Law and legislation —United States | Segregation —Law and legislation —United States | Equality before the law —United States | Minorities —Legal status, laws, etc. —France Classification: LCC KF4755 .W37 2025 (print) | LCC KF4755 (ebook) | DDC 342.7308/73 —dc23/eng/20250729 LC record available at https://lccn.loc.gov/2025034070 LC ebook record available at https://lccn.loc.gov/2025034071

ISBN: HB: 9781666961874
ePDF: 9798216254492
eBook: 9781978771598

Typeset by Deanta Global Publishing Services, Chennai, India

Contents

Introduction

This book contains a collection of essays that address many of the major race and equality controversies that were involved in Supreme Court cases and in other contexts. Throughout the twentieth century, and during the first decades of the twenty-first century, African Americans and other people of color have pursued an elusive quest for racial justice. An examination of the current status of African American families reveals a mixed picture: the best of times for some, the worst of times for others. For those in a position to take advantage of the opportunities created by the Civil Rights revolution of the 1960s, the gains over the last generation have been remarkable. For those left behind in America's impoverished communities, the obstacles to advancement are more daunting today than they were a generation ago. They continue to be plagued by the many issues arising from poverty and residential segregation.

Reconstruction

The first chapter of this book examines the Reconstruction Era. After the conclusion of the Civil War in 1865, three important amendments to the US Constitution were enacted. These included the Thirteenth Amendment, which outlawed slavery and involuntary servitude; the Fourteenth Amendment, which made the formerly enslaved people citizens; and the Fifteenth Amendment, which extended the franchise to former slaves, allowing them to vote and participate in the electoral process. During this period, African Americans held several elected positions in state and local governments in Southern states.

However, a series of Supreme Court decisions undermined the rights and protections that were granted by the Constitution. In Southern states, laws were enacted that disenfranchised Black voters and approved racial segregation. By the end of the nineteenth century, the Fourteenth and Fifteenth Amendments were nullified in the South.

The NAACPs' Legal Strategy

In the early decades of the twentieth century organizations were established that fought to restore the civil rights of African Americans. The best known of these, the NAACP, embarked on a campaign of lobbying and public education. In the early 1930s, the organization launched a long-range, carefully orchestrated legal strategy that was aimed at eliminating segregation in public education. These efforts culminated in the 1954 decision in *Brown v. Board of Education*, which held that segregation in public education violated the Equal Protection Clause of the Constitution.

The Southern states reacted to *Brown* with an official policy of "massive resistance." For the next fifteen years, very little progress was made in the efforts to desegregate schools. In the late 1960s, the Supreme Court held that Southern states were obligated to desegregate their schools. During the following twenty years, busing became the primary means to achieve student population integration. States were obligated to prove that they had eliminated all vestiges of segregation "root and branch."

In the 1990s, the Supreme Court relaxed the standard for determining whether the South's schools were integrated. Because school districts tend to be organized along the borders of local municipalities, student populations reflect the residential segregation that persists in most urban communities. Surveys show that schools are still *de facto* segregated. By the 2020–21 school year, more than a third of students attended predominantly same-race schools.

Racial Messages in Presidential Campaigns

For many years, elected officials have used racial bias to win elections. Implicit racial appeals avoid direct references to Black inferiority. They convey a subtle racial message by submerging it in nonracial content. The racial message is usually so subtle that many of its recipients are not aware of the source. Politicians have been able to exploit racial resentment using code words that avoid overt references to race.

Ronald Reagan's best-known effort was a story about a Chicago "welfare queen" who drove a Cadillac, had eighty aliases, thirty addresses, twelve Social Security cards, and collected benefits, defrauding the government of over $150,000. George H. W. Bush's 1988 campaign used images of Willie Horton, a convicted murderer, who kidnapped a young couple, stabbed the man and repeatedly raped his girlfriend. Horton's race was never mentioned, but his image activated the stereotype of a dangerous Black criminal. Mitt Romney's ads alluded to the stereotype of lazy African Americans relying on welfare benefits instead of working to earn a living.

When Donald Trump announced his candidacy, his speech was crafted to provoke the maximum effect. Dropping the subtle "dog whistle" tactic of previous campaigns, Trump picked up a megaphone. He called Mexicans "rapists" and criminals who bring drugs across the border. He said when Mexico sends its people, they are bringing drugs and crime. These pronouncements provoked extreme anti-immigrant sentiments, and they were successful.

The Migrant Crisis and the Rise of the Right

The final two chapters examine the impact of Europe's migrant crisis on political parties. Anti-immigrant sentiments are driving the rise of extreme right-wing political parties in Western Europe. The influx of ethnic minority immigrants from North Africa, Asia, and the Middle East is one of the main reasons for the rise of far-right parties. Native populations are motivated by a desire to preserve their countries from what they view as the corrosive effects of globalization and migration.

The central theme of ethnic nationalists is that nations are defined by a shared heritage, a common language, a common faith, and a shared ethnic ancestry. In France, Germany, Austria, the Scandinavian countries, and elsewhere in Europe, candidates running on ethnic nationalist platforms have made significant inroads in governing bodies. The main driver of the anti-immigration movement in Europe is the symbolic threat that immigrants present to national cultures and values.

1

Reconstruction

The Reconstruction era implemented by Congress, which lasted from 1866 to 1877, was aimed at reorganizing the Southern states after the Civil War, providing the means for readmitting them into the Union, and defining the means by which whites and Blacks could live together in society. During the years after the war, Black and white teachers from the North and South, missionary organizations, churches, and schools worked to give the emancipated population the opportunity to learn.

After the Civil War, with the protections of the Thirteenth, Fourteenth, and Fifteenth Amendments to the Constitution and the Civil Rights Act of 1866, African Americans enjoyed a period when they were allowed to vote, actively participate in the political process, acquire the land of former owners, seek their own employment, and use public accommodations. African Americans became involved in the political process as voters and as governmental representatives at the local, state, and national levels.

Sixteen Blacks served in Congress. African Americans also held hundreds of other elective offices at the state and local levels. Missionary societies and northern philanthropists established a network of educational institutions throughout the South for Blacks. At the state level, eighteen African Americans served as lieutenant governor, treasurer, superintendent of schools, and Secretary of State.

A number of important measures were enacted. One of them, the Civil Rights Act of 1866, states:

> all persons born in the United States . . . are hereby declared to be citizens of the United States; and such citizens, of every race and color, without regard to any previous condition of slavery or involuntary servitude . . . shall have the same right . . . to make and enforce contracts, to sue, be parties, and give

> evidence, to inherit, purchase, lease, sell, hold, and convey real and personal property, and to full and equal benefit of all laws and proceedings for the security of person and property, as is enjoyed by white citizens.[1]

During the same year, Congress enacted the Fourteenth Amendment of the Constitution. It states, "No state shall make or enforce any law which shall abridge the privileges or immunities of citizens of the United States; nor shall any state deprive any person of life, liberty, or property, without due process of law; nor deny to any person within its jurisdiction the equal protection of the laws."

In 1869, the Fifteenth Amendment granted the franchise: "The right of citizens of the United States to vote shall not be denied or abridged by the United States or by any state on account of race, color, or previous condition of servitude."

Finally, the Civil Rights Act of 1875 states:

> all persons within the jurisdiction of the United States shall be entitled to the full and equal enjoyment of the accommodations, advantages, facilities, and privileges of inns, public conveyances on land or water, theaters, and other places of public amusement; subject only to the conditions and limitations established by law, and applicable alike to citizens of every race and color, regardless of any previous condition of servitude.[2]

Reconstruction ended with the Hayes-Tilden Compromise of 1877[3]. No candidate received an undisputed majority; the election was decided by the electoral commission. A compromise was struck in which former Confederate officials were allowed to participate in the political process in southern states. Federal troops were withdrawn from the South. White Southerners reasserted their predominance. Secret societies such as the Ku Klux Klan were established. A reign of domestic terrorism prevailed. Between 1884 and 1920, white mobs lynched more than 3,000 Blacks in the South. Black officeholders were beaten and murdered; their houses were burned, and Black voters were prevented from casting ballots.

During the last decades of the nineteenth century, the Supreme Court issued a series of decisions that considerably undermined the efficacy of the Fifteenth and Fourteenth Amendments. In *United States v. Reese*,[4]a Black man residing in Kentucky attempted to vote, but his poll tax payment was rejected, and he was turned away from the poll. The Supreme Court rejected his challenge, holding that the Fourteenth Amendment did not affirmatively assure the right to vote. The amendment merely prohibited states from denying it.

United States v. *Cruikshank*[5] involved a massacre in Colfax, Louisiana. On April 13, more than 300 armed white men attacked the courthouse. When the militia maneuvered a cannon to fire on the courthouse, some of the Black defenders fled while others surrendered. When the leader of the attackers, James Hadnot, was accidentally shot by one of his own men, the white militia responded by shooting the Black prisoners. Those who were wounded in the earlier battle were singled out for execution.

Approximately 150 African Americans were killed, including forty-eight who were murdered after the battle. A total of ninety-seven white militia men were arrested and charged with violations of the Enforcement Act of 1870. A handful of them were convicted but were eventually released in 1875. The Supreme Court reversed their convictions and held the exercise the franchise was not an attribute of "national citizenship" under the Fourteenth Amendment. The parties had not established that they were denied any rights based on their race. Historian Eric Foner described the massacre as the worst episodes of racial violence during the Reconstruction era.

In the *Civil Rights Cases* of 1883,[6] key provisions of the 1875 Reconstruction Civil Rights Act were declared unconstitutional. Suits filed by Black citizens claimed they had been illegally refused access to restaurants, hotels, theaters, and trains in violation of the Civil Rights Act of 1875. The decision established the "state action" doctrine, holding that Congress did not have the authority to regulate private acts of discrimination. The court concluded, referring to African Americans, that "there must be some stage in the progress of his elevation when he takes the rank of a mere citizen and ceases to be a special favorite of the law."[7]

In *Williams v. Mississippi*[8] the US Supreme Court in 1898 upheld a poll tax, disenfranchisement clauses, literacy tests, and a grandfather clause, all of which were features of the 1890 Mississippi Constitution and statutes. The Mississippi state Constitutional convention had the express purpose of disenfranchising Black voters. The delegates added a poll tax that precluded persons from voting if they had been convicted of various petty crimes.

The new Mississippi Constitution also contained an "understanding clause." Black voters were tested on arcane materials while semiliterate whites were asked only to read their name or some other simple text. The constitutional provisions were not facially discriminatory but that was the express intent of legislators. When the Constitution was challenged, the Supreme Court ignored the legislature's intent. It ruled that because Mississippi's Constitution was not expressly discriminatory, it did not violate the Equal Protection Clause of the Fourteenth Amendment.

In the post-Reconstruction period, an unprecedented reign of violence and domestic terrorism prevailed across the South. One striking example occurred in 1898 when a mob of white Supremacists attacked and overthrew the duly elected municipal government in Wilmington, North Carolina. In the 1890s, Wilmington was North Carolina's most populous city. It had a busy commercial port and a strong economy. A majority of its citizens were Black. It had a thriving Black middle class made up of both professionals and entrepreneurs.

Black citizens were employed as artisans, industrial workers, laborers, members of maritime crews, and domestic workers. Three of the city's aldermen were Black. Of the five members on the board of audit and finance, one was African Americans also served in the civic positions including justice of the peace, deputy clerk of court, street superintendent, and as coroners, policemen, mail clerks, and mail carriers.

In the days preceding the 1898 election, Alfred Moore Waddell, a former Confederate officer and US Congressman, proposed the removal of the Republicans and Populists then in power in Wilmington. He proclaimed in a speech that the white citizens, if necessary, would "choke the Cape Fear with carcasses." [9] Waddell and other whites were inflamed by the publication of an editorial in the Daily Record, a local Black-owned newspaper.

Alex Manly, the editor of *Daily Record*, charged that "poor white men are careless in the matter of protecting their women" and that "our experience among poor white people in the country teaches us that women of that race are not any more particular in the matter of clandestine meetings with colored men than the white men with colored women." One of America's oldest and most enduring taboos is Black males having sexual relations with white females. Manly's editorial, reprinted across the state, provided Democrats with an issue that inflamed racial tensions as Election Day approached.

Nothing happened on election day, but two days later about 500 white men assembled at the armory of the Wilmington Light Infantry. Waddell led the group to the Daily Record office. The crowd swelled to as many as 2,000 as they moved across town. Manly Blacks fled the city, as had numerous other Blacks anticipating violence. The mob invaded the building. After a fire broke out, the top floor was consumed. Within hours, violence had spread to other parts of the city. An untold number of Blacks were killed. Hundreds fled the city.

Local elected officials were forced to resign and were replaced by white supremacist leaders. Silas P. Wright, the white Republican mayor, resigned at gunpoint. Waddell took office as mayor and held the office until 1905. The revolt had the support of many of the most powerful men in the city. A state legislative committee was convened that sponsored a poll tax and a "Grandfather Clause," stating that those who had enjoyed the right to vote prior to 1866 or 1867 and their lineal descendants would be exempt from educational, property, or tax requirements for voting.

A turning point in the history of segregation was "the Atlanta compromise." This was a speech delivered to a largely white audience at Atlanta's Piedmont Park on September 18, 1895, by Booker T. Washington, founder of Tuskegee University. The Atlanta compromise proposed an understanding between African Americans and Southern white leaders. Invoking a powerful metaphor, Washington said, "In all things that are purely social we can be as separate as the fingers, yet one as the hand in all things essential to mutual progress."[10] The idea was that Southern Blacks would provide labor for white employers, acquiesce to segregation, and submit to white political rule. In return, Northern philanthropists would support Black educational charities, such as the Tuskegee Institute in Alabama.

The crowd responded with thunderous applause. The governor of Georgia, who was sitting on the platform, rushed over to shake Washington's hand. Newspapers across the nation printed the speech. President Grover Cleveland telegraphed a note of congratulations from his summer home in Cape Cod,

Massachusetts. The Atlanta compromise was seen as the solution to the problems the South experienced during the Reconstruction era. Washington was launched to an unprecedented position of international fame and unparalleled influence. Appointments to any position of importance required Washington's approval.

The Atlanta Compromise set the stage for *Plessy v. Ferguson*.[11] In this 1896 decision, the Supreme Court accorded legal sanction to the doctrine of "separate but equal." The case involved a Louisiana statute which required railroad carriers to provide "equal but separate" accommodations for the white and the colored races. Persons violating the statute were subject to fine or imprisonment. A group of Louisiana Creoles organized a challenge to the ordinance. They selected Homer Plessy, who was 7/8 Caucasian and 1/8 African but not discernibly Black, to serve as the plaintiff. He was, as one commentator observed, light enough to gain access to the coach but dark enough to be ejected for violating the segregation ordinance.

Plessy was directed to the coach reserved for colored passengers. After refusing to obey the conductor's directive, Plessy was forcibly ejected from the train and arrested for violating the segregation ordinance. A suit was filed. When a case came to trial, Plessy argued that the Louisiana statute violated the Thirteenth and Fourteenth Amendments of the US Constitution. The case eventually made its way to the Supreme Court.

Speaking for the majority, Justice Brown dismissed the Thirteenth Amendment almost summarily. That amendment, he found, was enacted to abolish slavery and other forms of involuntary servitude. A law which established a legal distinction between the races did not, in his view, deny legal equality for the races or reestablish involuntary servitude. Turning to the Fourteenth Amendment, Justice Brown cited a series of earlier cases, including one allowing racially segregated schools in Boston, as authority for permitting states to enact statutes which made distinctions based on race. According to the majority:

> the enforced separation of races . . . neither abridges or privileges or immunities of the colored man, deprives him of his property without due process of law, nor denies him equal protection of the laws, within the meaning of the Fourteenth Amendment.[12]

Plessy also argued that there was a deprivation of a property interest involved in racial classifications. The Court responded that if this were so, it would occur only if a white passenger were assigned to a coach designated to serve Black passengers. In such a case, the white passenger might have an action for damages against the railroad. In the reverse situation, a Black passenger would not have a claim because there would be no harm caused by contact with white passengers. Plessy argued further that the statute allowing classifications based on color could be taken to absurd extremes. For example, if racial segregation were permitted, it could be invoked to justify regulations requiring segregated sidewalks, painting a white man's house white and Black persons houses Black or different colored signs on places of business depending upon the race of the owner.

The majority rejected this argument after it found that classification would have to be reasonable. Arbitrary classifications such as those suggested by Plessy would not satisfy the standard of reasonableness. Segregation did not, in the majority's view, stigmatize the Black race or stamp it with a badge of inferiority. If this were so, it would by reason of anything found in the act but solely based on the colored race's choice to put that construction on it. The majority echoed the then prevailing view that social prejudice could not be overcome by legislation. If the two races were to meet on terms and social equality, it must be the result of natural affinities and mutual appreciation of each other's merits and a voluntary consent of the individuals. "If one race be inferior to the other socially, the Constitution of the United States cannot put them on the same plane."

In what became one of the best-known dissents in the history of the Supreme Court, Justice John Marshall Harlan argued that the Thirteenth Amendment prohibited slavery and prevented the imposition of any burdens that amounted to a badge of slavery. Harlan contended that the amendment granted Blacks the right to exemption from any legislation against them based on color. Recognizing the actual intent of the ordinance, Harlan explained that the law was not intended to exclude white persons from railroad cars occupied by Blacks but to prevent Black persons from occupying cars reserved for white passengers.

In the most remembered passage of the opinion, Justice Harlan argued that "our Constitution is colorblind and neither knows nor tolerates classes among citizens." He concluded by predicting that "the judgment rendered this day will be will prove to be as pernicious as the decision made by this tribunal in the Dred Scott case."

After the Supreme Court's endorsement in *Plessy v. Ferguson*, racial separation was imposed on virtually all aspects of everyday life in the South. Whites and Blacks were born in separate hospitals, educated in different schools, and buried in segregated graveyards. Schools, restaurants, hotels, theaters, public transportation, and waiting rooms were segregated, as were elevators, parks, public restrooms, hospitals, drinking fountains, prisons, and places of worship. Segregated waiting rooms were required in professional offices, as well as building entrances and cemeteries. Amusement parks had separate cashier windows.

Local ordinances forbade African Americans from living in white neighborhoods. Segregation was enforced for public pools, phone booths, asylums, jails, and homes for the elderly and disabled. The labor market was segmented. There were white jobs and Black jobs; men's work and women's work. African Americans were domestics, janitors, laborers, and the like. These were the lowest-paying and least desirable occupations. New Orleans mandated the segregation of prostitutes according to race. In Atlanta, African Americans testifying in court cases were sworn in using a different Bible than whites. Marriage and cohabitation between whites and Blacks were strictly forbidden in most Southern states. "Sundown towns" were not uncommon; signs were posted at city limits warning African Americans that they were not welcome there.[13]

All branches of the US military were segregated. In 1913, President Woodrow Wilson segregated the federal Civil Service.[14] In 1915, he screened D. W. Griffith's *Birth of a Nation* in the White House. The movie glorified the Ku Klux Klan and portrayed Blacks as ignorant brutes. Wilson supposedly said, "It's like writing history with lightning. And my only regret is that it is all terribly true."[15] Segregation was codified in state and local laws and enforced by intimidation and violence. There were, in effect, two criminal justice systems: one for whites and another for Blacks. When the color line was breached, violence was unleashed against offenders by the Ku Klux Klan and local whites; often in concert with local law enforcement officials.

In Atlanta, Georgia, Blacks could not serve on juries. The races were indexed separately on tax rolls. Atlanta's banks maintained separate teller windows for white and Black customers. The Rhodes-Haverty building in Atlanta had four elevators. Three for whites and one for Blacks. All four elevators going down were integrated. The apparent logic was that whites and Blacks go to separate heavens but the same hell.[16]

Blacks could not try on clothes in department stores. They were expected to wait until all of the white customers were served before they were helped. Jim Crow etiquette was scrupulously observed in interactions. Blacks were expected to address a white person by the title of "Mr." "Mrs." or "Miss." Whites addressed Blacks by their first names no matter if they hardly knew each other or by the epithets "boy," "uncle," "auntie," or the like. If a Black person entered a white person's home, they were obligated to use the back door. The purpose of these unwritten but well-known rules was to provide a continual demonstration that Blacks were inferior to whites and recognized their inferiority.[17]

When *Plessy* was decided, the collective anti-Black sentiment was such that very few white Americans gave any serious consideration to the equality of African Americans. Theories of "scientific" racism that purported to prove Black inferiority were widespread in the nineteenth century. Samuel Morton, a professor of medicine at the University of Pennsylvania, claimed that differences in head shapes could predict a racial group's intelligence and other personality traits. Morton's theory of Polygenesis also hypothesized that racial groups did not share a common origin. This provided a "scientific" basis for viewing African-descended people as different and inferior species.[18]

Eugenics was introduced in the late nineteenth century by Francis Galton, a British scientist who theorized that the traits and behaviors of humans could be predicted and controlled by breeding people with the "best" genes. Phrenology was another popular theory. Adherents believed that personality traits and characteristics could be ascertained by measuring the shape of an individual's head. Combating these beliefs would prove to be a formidable task.

Groups were organized to fight segregation A large-scale assault on the Black residents of Springfield, Illinois, was the precipitating factor in the birth of the National Association for the Advancement of Colored People (NAACP).[19] In mid-August 1908, the white population of Springfield, Illinois, violently reacted to reports that a white woman had been assaulted in her home by a Black man. Soon afterwards, another assault by a Black man on a white woman was reported. Springfield police arrested an African American, Joe James, for one of the assaults. Another man, George Richardson, a local factory worker, was arrested for the second assault. A mob that had been forming assembled at the county courthouse to lynch the two men in custody.

Unable to get the accused men who had been moved to an undisclosed location, the mob turned its anger on two other Black men who were quickly lynched. The mob attacked the homes of Black families in Springfield and extended their violence into small communities outside the city limits. Some Springfield Blacks fought back in self-defense. When the carnage finally ended, six Black people were shot and killed, two were lynched, and hundreds of thousands of dollars' worth of property was destroyed. About two thousand Black people were driven out of Springfield.

The violence at Springfield was not an isolated incident. It was merely one of several episodes of brutality directed by white mobs against Black communities. What many found alarming was the fact that they occurred outside of the South in the birthplace of Abraham Lincoln. Many worried that the "race war" in the South would be transported to northern cities. These events prompted Mary Ovington, a social worker active in a number of organizations, to contact William English Walling, a sociologist who supported progressive causes, and Dr. Henry Moscowitz, another well-known progressive. The group issued a "call" for the formation of a radical movement that would develop a program aimed at securing racial equality for African Americans.

A steering committee was formed and a conference was convened in New York City on May 31, 1909. Within a year, a committee was created to establish a permanent organization.[20] By this time, the organizers had decided to name their organization the National Association for the Advancement of Colored People. A conference of the newly formed NAACP was held on May 12–14, 1910, in New York City. At this meeting, the organization's goals were outlined and officers were elected. Morefield Story of Boston was elected to serve as president. William English Walling of New York agreed to chair the executive committee. John B. Mulholland of New York was designated treasurer, and Oswald Garrison Villard was designated disbursing treasurer. W. E. B. Du Bois was appointed to serve as director of publicity and research. Francis Blascoer was selected to serve as the executive secretary.

Immediately after his decision to join the NAACP, Du Bois began to assemble a publication to support the organization's objectives. In November of 1911, *The Crisis* was prepared for distribution. Approximately 1,000 copies were printed. The magazine was well received, as Du Bois observed later, "the magazine came at the psychological moment and its success was phenomenal."

The NAACP grew rapidly. By 1913, the NAACP had established branch offices in cities across the nation. Membership grew rapidly, from around 9,000 in 1917 to approximately 90,000 in 1919, with more than 300 local branches. Among the Association's top priorities was eradicating lynching. Throughout a thirty-year campaign, the NAACP waged legislative battles, gathered and published crucial statistics, organized mass protests, and produced artistic material urging the end of anti-Black violence.

Notes

1 42 U.S.C. §§ 1981–1982 (1987).

2 M.I. Urofsky, Civil Rights Act of 1875. *Encyclopedia Britannica*, Feb. 23, 2024. https://www.britannica.com/topic/Civil-Rights-Act-United-States-1875.

3 History, Compromise of 1877.

4 *United States v. Reese*, 92 US 214 (1876).

5 *United States v. Cruikshank* 92 US 542 (1875).

6 *Civil Rights Cases* , 109 US 3 (1883).

7 *Civil Rights Cases* 109 US 3 (1883).

8 *Williams v. Mississippi*, 170 US 213 (1898).

9 Aaron Randle, *America's Only Successful Coup d'Etat Overthrew a Biracial Government* in 1898. history.com/news/wilmington-massacre-1898-coup.

10 Louis R. Harlan, *Booker T. Washington: The Making of a Black Leader, 1856–1901,* (Oxford University Press, Feb. 13, 1975).

11 *Plessy v. Ferguson*, 163 US 537 (1896).
12 *Plessy*, 163 US 537.
13 James Loewen, *Sundown Towns: A Hidden Dimension of American Racism* (Touchstone, 2006).
14 Eric S. Yellin, *Racism in the Nation's Service: Government Workers and the Color Line in Woodrow Wilson's America* (2013).
15 Mark E. Benbow, *Birth of a Quotation: Woodrow Wilson and 'Like Writing History with Lightning,'* 9(4) JGAPE 509–33 (2010). http://www.jstor.org/stable/20799409.
16 Gary Pomerantz, *Where Peachtree Meets Sweet Auburn: A Saga of Race and Family* (Penguin Books, 1997); Reprint edition; Frank Ruechel, *New Deal Public Housing, Urban Poverty, and Jim Crow: Techwood and University Homes in Atlanta*, 81(4) GHQ 915–37 (1997). http://www.jstor.org/stable/40550189.
17 Gunnar Myrdal, *An American Dilemma: The Negro Problem and Modern Democracy* (1944).
18 Samuel George Morton, *Crania Americana.*
19 Springfield Race Riot, www.britannica.com/event/Springfield-Race-Riot.
20 https://naacp.org/about/our-history.

2

Public Schools and the Shaping of the American Identity

By the end of the nineteenth century, the Fourteenth and Fifteenth Amendments were all but nullified in the South. In the North and South, African Americans were confined to substandard housing in segregated neighborhoods and excluded from all but the lowest paying, least desirable occupations. This history, which is America's enduring paradox, had a significant effect on the development of the American identity. Most of the rights and obligations of American citizens are based on state, rather than federal, laws. Public schools are established by states and governed primarily by state laws. School districts are political subdivisions of state governments. Schools are operated by elected governing boards and financed primarily by local property taxes.

Pedagogical practices are determined by each local district. States license teachers, set certification standards, and provide financial assistance to local districts. The federal government provides financial assistance mainly through categorical grants that are conditioned upon the states and local school boards' agreement to develop programs that reflect educational priorities set by Congress. To receive federal funding, states and local districts have aligned the content of programmatic offerings and special services with federal priorities.

Apart from a common language, there has never been one set of cultural values that shape a shared identity for all Americans. The Declaration of Independence speaks broadly of certain "fundamental truths," but that document was intended to benefit white male property owners, many of whom owned African slaves. America is a republic consisting of fifty, quasi-sovereign states. The nation has always had a myriad of different religions with different, and sometimes conflicting, tenets.

The America of the imagination is a nation of white, English-speaking descendants of immigrants from Western Europe whose values and traditions are based on Anglo-Saxon cultural norms.[1] With the exception of the indigenous Native Americans, our ancestors migrated not only from Europe but Asia, Africa, South America, and other localities across the globe. They represent many religious and cultural traditions.

The system of racial segregation isolated the African American population, forcing it to develop its own set of values and traditions. Efforts to desegregate public schools in America have been complicated by the different, and sometimes conflicting, cultural perspectives of whites, African Americans, and other racial minorities. Given this diversity, what are, or should be, the "cultural values" that are inculcated by America's public schools?

Culture is the distinctive spiritual, material, intellectual, and emotional features of a social group encompassing its art, literature, value systems, traditions, and beliefs. It includes the values and behaviors shared by the group. American culture is based largely on Western European norms. It has been influenced to some extent by native peoples, Africans brought to the United States as slaves, and other more recent immigrants from Latin America, Asia, the Caribbean, and elsewhere, but the predominant influence has always been Western European.

Much of American culture is based on the ideals of the Enlightenment. The Declaration of Independence, for example, emphasizes the importance of "life, liberty, and the pursuit of happiness." The ideals of liberty and individual rights are embedded in the US Constitution's Bill of Rights. These principles shaped the nation's economic, political, and social development. Educational institutions, particularly public schools, have had a central role in inculcating American identity and culture in succeeding generations.

Public schools in America can be traced to the colonial era, before the Revolutionary War. When he served in Virginia's General Assembly, Thomas Jefferson proposed a system of public schools which would have provided three years of public schooling for all children and advanced education for a select few. This would, as Jefferson put it, "rak[e] a few geniuses from the rubbish." Jefferson's efforts to persuade Virginia's legislature to establish public schools failed, but he eventually led the successful effort to create the state-supported University of Virginia.

The development of public schools in America began in Massachusetts primarily through the work and influence of Horace Mann.[2] In 1837, Mann became the first secretary of the Massachusetts Board of Education. Mann soon realized the need for public support for education. He inspected the schools across the state and found large disparities in the facilities and programs of instruction.

Mann held meetings in which he promoted the creation of a system of "common schools." These would be tuition-free public schools that provided quality instruction. Standards would be set and enforced at the state level, and the entire system would be funded with tax dollars. Common schools would serve both males and females and would teach a common body of knowledge. Mann described his vision:

> It is a free school system, it knows no distinction of rich and poor . . . it throws open its doors and spreads the table of its bounty for all children in the state . . . Education then, beyond all other devices of human origin, is an equalizer of the conditions of men, the great balance wheel of the social machinery.[3]

As a result of Mann's efforts, a training school for teachers was established in Lexington, Massachusetts, in 1839. Mann successfully advocated the establishment of free libraries. He persuaded officials to increase teacher salaries; school committees were compensated, new schools were built, and state aid to education increased. By the Civil War, all of the northeastern states established departments of education, teacher training programs, and tax-supported public schools. Identity took on an increasing importance with the arrival of waves of European immigrants.

By 1840, nearly half of New York City's residents were immigrants, many of whom were Irish Catholics. Irish Catholic children attended schools where the King James Bible was read, Protestant hymns were sung, and Protestant prayers were recited. The orientation of the teaching was typically Protestant and often anti-Irish and anti-Catholic. Catholics became increasingly uncomfortable with the ethnic and religious bias in New York City's schools. They demanded that city funds be made available for parochial schools.

This request was met with strenuous opposition. Opponents argued that allowing Catholics a portion of the public-school funds would lead to a flood of requests from other religious denominations. At times the conflict escalated into violence. In 1844 a Catholic church in Pennsylvania was burned, killing thirteen people in what became known as the "Philadelphia Bible riots." John Hughes was named Archbishop of New York in 1850. He was the leader in an effort that created a privately funded national system of Catholic schools, which eventually became the leading alternative to public schools.

As the Western regions of the United States were settled, rudimentary schools were established. Schools were seen as an attractive and stabilizing feature in isolated settlements. Many of the schools were run by women. Catherine Beecher, Harriet Beecher Stowe's sister, was a leader in efforts to promote the use of female teachers in the West. She also advocated teaching as a respectable occupation for middle-class women. This influenced many women from the Eastern states to travel for teaching positions.

Public schools were established in the Eastern and Midwestern regions of the US before and after the Civil War. The growth of these institutions escalated during the last half of the nineteenth century. School expenditures rose from 69 million dollars in 1870 to 147 million dollars in 1890. During the same period, school enrollments increased to 7.6 million students. By the end of the nineteenth century, the United States was providing more education to more children than any other nation.

By the beginning of the twentieth century, the United States was becoming more urban and ethnically diverse. Cities were growing in a rapidly industrializing nation. Manufacturing created a need for inexpensive labor. Waves of immigrants from Eastern and Southern Europe responded to that demand. Between 1890 and 1930, more than 22 million immigrants came to the United States. After they arrived and took jobs in factories and elsewhere, they enrolled their children in public schools.

During this period, John Dewey, a professor of philosophy at the University of Chicago, became an influential figure in public education.[4] He was a leading proponent of what became known as the progressive education movement. Dewey believed that common schools had become repressive institutions that did not adequately promote intellectual exploration and growth. Dewey and other progressive educators opposed those who promoted academic education for elites and vocational training for the masses.

Dewey argued that schools should teach students critical thinking and problem-solving skills rather than rote lessons. Dewey also believed that schools should help students interact with others. In addition to reading, writing, and arithmetic, progressive educators instructed immigrants in hygiene, manners, and home economics. Immigrant students also learned American styles of eating, dressing, and other cultural habits.

There were other forces that influenced public school education in the first decades of the twentieth century. Before the First World War the children of German immigrants were taught in their own language in places such as St. Louis, Cincinnati, and Cleveland. After the conclusion of the war, anti-German sentiments resulted in the enactment of laws requiring English-only instruction. Schools were prohibited from providing instruction in languages other than English, and they emphasized American customs and traditions.

During this period, an assimilationist paradigm was established. Educators facilitated the Americanization of immigrants by inculcating the values and traditions of an Anglo-Saxon culture. Customs, language, and other forms of cultural expressions from the "old country" were discarded. In public schools, good citizenship became more a matter of conforming to a middle-class pattern of behavior than questioning how the political system operated. Many schools required students to recite the Lord's Prayer and passages from the Bible. The school calendar was organized around Christian holidays such as Christmas and Easter. Other, more secular holidays, such as Thanksgiving, celebrated American traditions. Students pledged allegiance to the flag every morning, sang "America the Beautiful" at assemblies, and were taught from texts that extolled the virtues of the Founding Fathers.

African Americans and the Pedagogy of Subordination

During the final decades of the nineteenth century, a dual system of public education was established in the South: one for whites and another for Blacks. Instead of inculcating American culture and identity, the educational program for African Americans was predicated on political disenfranchisement, civic inequality, and racial segregation. Black students were trained to accept a subordinate status.

This approach to education is identified with the educational philosophy of Booker T. Washington, the Black educator who was the founder of Tuskegee Institute in Alabama. It was, however, a pedagogical model that was developed at Hampton Institute, the institution where Washington was educated. Hampton was a school established in Hampton, Virginia, to educate African American and Native American students. When Washington attended Hampton, it was neither a college nor a trade school; it was a normal school composed of elementary school graduates who were seeking some additional years of teacher-training courses so they could qualify for normal school teaching certificates. The Hampton Model envisioned the removal of Black voters and politicians from southern political life, the relegation of Black workers to the lowest levels of labor in the southern economy, and the perpetuation of a southern racial hierarchy.[5]

The Hampton Model was embraced by educational reformers who were supported by northern philanthropists. It was designed to produce unskilled and semiskilled Black workers who would provide inexpensive labor for the southern economy. The product of this training would be a diligent and reliable worker with an elementary education and industrial training. Manual labor, rather than scholarship, was the criterion for educational development.

Southern planters were skeptical about the value of any form of education. They were accustomed to a society in which Black laborers worked for them under a system of intimidation, violence, and compulsion. Social control rested on coercion. Most southerners believed that with intelligent direction, Blacks could be suitable and inexpensive laborers who could obey orders but were incapable of directing their own labor. General Samuel Armstrong, the founder of Hampton Institute, believed that training in agriculture and industry would give ex-slaves the skills needed for the economic advancement of the South. Armstrong argued that freedmen did not have the cultural and moral qualities necessary to take part in politics and should not vote. This philosophy made Armstrong's educational program acceptable to Southern whites.

In 1895, Washington stood on a platform in what is now a park in Atlanta, Georgia. He addressed a large and mainly white audience at the Cotton States Exposition. Washington shared the platform with a distinguished group that included the governor of Georgia. During his speech, Washington invoked a powerful metaphor that would be seen as the solution for race relations in the South.

Extending a hand toward the audience, Washington stated, "[i]n all things purely social we can be as separate as the fingers, yet as one hand in all things essential to mutual progress."[6] The crowd responded with enthusiastic applause, and the governor of Georgia rushed over to shake Washington's hand. Newspapers across the nation carried accounts of the remarks. President Grover Cleveland telegraphed a congratulatory note. After the speech, Washington's position as the preeminent leader of Black America was secured.

As Washington delivered his Atlanta address, a test case orchestrated by a group of African Americans in New Orleans, Louisiana, was on its way to the Supreme Court. The case challenged a local ordinance that required segregation on railroads. The plaintiff, Homer Plessy, argued that the ordinance violated the Fourteenth and Thirteenth Amendments to the Constitution because it treated Black passengers differently and less favorably than white passengers. Plessy and his supporters were confident that their challenge would succeed.

In 1896, however, the Supreme Court decided that the enforced separation of the races ". . . neither abridges the privileges or immunities of the colored man, deprives him of this property without due process of law nor denies him equal protection of the law within the meaning of the Fourteenth Amendment." The Court stated that "[i]f one race be inferior to the other socially, the Constitution of the United States cannot put them on the same plane."[7]

Plessy endorsed racial segregation and established the "separate-but-equal" doctrine. The Court held that laws requiring segregation did not violate the Fourteenth Amendment if the separate facilities provided for Blacks were equal to those available to whites. Accommodations for African Americans were always separate but hardly equal.

Washington and his supporters were able to persuade Southerners that their educational program would produce a more productive and content labor force. They convinced southern planters and northern philanthropists that their system would improve the health, morals, and efficiency of Black workers and would socialize Black youth to the discipline and values needed to maintain race and class relations.

Training Black teachers for normal schools was a critical feature in the development of the economic and social structure. Black teachers were influential and highly regarded in the African American community. White educational leaders recognized that teachers would be critical to shaping the social, economic, and political consciousness of the Black masses. The Hampton-Tuskegee model would be propagated to the Black masses by Black teachers.

Conclusion

After the ascendancy of Booker T. Washington and the success of Tuskegee Institute, the Hampton-Tuskegee model was embraced by public school officials throughout the South. It was reflected in the course offerings available in Black schools. School curricula prepared students for careers as cooks, maids, laundresses, porters, chauffeurs, and the like. African Americans were intended to occupy the lowest paying, least desirable occupations. Washington's pedagogy of subordination was sustained until it was challenged by the litigation campaign that culminated in *Brown v. Board of Education.*[8]

Notes

1 Nathanael O'Reilly J., Imagined America: Walt Whitman's Nationalism in the First Edition of Leaves of Grass, *IJAS Online*, Jun. 29, 2009.

2 James D. Anderson, *Education of Backs in the South 1860–1835* (1988); Michael T. Nettles and Lara W. Perla, *The Frederick D Patterson Research Institute of College fund/United Negro College Fund.* The African-American Education Databook volume II Preschool through High School Education.

3 *Life and Complete Works of Horace Mann* (2 vols., Cambridge, 1869).

4 Hildebrand, David, "John Dewey," The Stanford Encyclopedia of Philosophy (Summer 2024 Edition), Edward N. Zalta & Uri Nodelman (eds.), https://plato.stanford.edu/archives/sum2024/entries/dewey/.

5 https://www.cambridge.org/core/books/abs/cambridge-guide-to-african-american-history/hamptontuskegee-idea/155FA726E97D8D697CAF37CD69A95EEE#.

6 T. Britannica, Editors of Encyclopaedia. 'Atlanta Compromise,' *Encyclopedia Britannica*, Jul. 27, 2020. https://www.britannica.com/event/Atlanta-Compromise.

7 *Plessy v. Ferguson*, 163 US 537 (1896).

8 *Brown v. Board of Education of Topeka*, 347 US 483 (1954).

3

The Equalization Strategy

An event that would have a major impact on the direction of the NAACP occurred in 1922 when Charles Garland, the son of a Boston millionaire, donated $800,000 to establish a fund to support radical causes. The Garland fund was administered by a group of liberal activists that included James Weldon Johnson, executive secretary of the NAACP, Roger Baldwin, the founder of the American Civil Liberties Union, Morris Ernest, Louis Garland, and Norman Thomas.[1]

Garland turned his inheritance over with the request that it be given away as quickly as possible to support unpopular causes without regard to race, creed, or color. In 1929, Johnson, Gannett, and Ernest established the Committee on Negro Work to focus on the problems of Black Americans. The committee eventually drafted a proposal recommending the award of a grant to the NAACP to carry out a large-scale campaign to secure the constitutional rights of southern Blacks. The proposal went through numerous drafts, which emphasized various approaches, but it ultimately considered a request for funds to finance a series of taxpayer lawsuits that would challenge the denial of constitutional rights that African Americans were enduring as a result of racial segregation.

The proposal was not greeted with unanimous approval. The most vocal opponent, Roger Baldwin, the founder of the American Civil Liberties Union, doubted the likelihood of the success of a litigation program. Baldwin's objection appeared to have been based on ideological grounds. Like many leftists and radicals, he did not believe that the court system, an inherently conservative institution, could be used to effect the sort of fundamental changes that would be needed to obtain the rights of African Americans.

Baldwin's views reflected the ideological views of other leftists, which would come into conflict with the NAACP on some occasions. Baldwin and other radicals viewed race relations in the 1920s and 1930s as the components of the class struggle between capitalists and workers. Equal rights for Black Americans were merely one aspect of an overall struggle by the oppressed masses to secure their freedom. Expressing his reservation to a friend Baldwin sent a copy of the proposal stating his personal view that the program should be approached from an economic standpoint. Despite the continuing resistance mounted by Baldwin and others, the Garland Fund eventually approved a grant for $100,000. Walter White succeeded Johnson as Executive Secretary of the NAACP in 1931. The Garland grant was announced after his appointment with an explanation that it was intended to assist in an intense campaign against specific handicaps burdening African Americans, including unequal apportionment of school funds, barring African Americans from juries, Jim Crow laws, residential segregation caused by restrictive covenants, disenfranchisement, and civil liberties defense.

The NAACP decided to hire a lawyer to review the laws that discriminated against African Americans and develop a legal strategy to attack discrimination and segregation. White ultimately selected Nathan Margold, a Harvard graduate. He eventually prepared what became known as the Margold Report. The document included an analysis of the constitutional foundation for the separate but equal doctrine and recommended a legal strategy to attack segregation. After analyzing the turn-of-the-century decisions, the report worked its way through the laws governing segregation up to 1931. Margold suggested a means by which legal obstacles might be overcome. He confirmed that the separate but equal doctrine as practiced was decidedly separate but hardly equal. In public schools, for example, there were glaring inequalities in the resources allocated to white schools compared to those provided for Black schools.[2]

Margold's main conclusion was that segregation as practiced was unconstitutional even if the *Plessy* rationale were accepted. The system was, in reality, segregation coupled with discrimination. Margold argued that if the NAACP boldly challenged the constitutional validity of segregation when coupled irredeemably with discrimination, the organization could strike directly at the most prolific sources of discrimination. In the key conclusion, Margold argued that segregation coupled with discrimination resulting from administrative action is just as much in denial of equal protection as is segregation required by express statutory authority.

Margold submitted his report to the NAACP in 1931, but a few years would pass before the organization could act on his suggestions. By that time, the prospect of receiving the $100,000 originally promised had nearly evaporated as a result of losses during the Depression.

At the time the NAACP was considering a litigation program, W. E. B. Du Bois wrote an editorial in 1934 that set off a firestorm within the NAACP. The uproar ultimately led to Du Bois' resignation from the organization. The article, "Segregation," reflected a dramatic departure from the NAACP's integrationist philosophy. Du Bois argued that African Americans should adopt a program of self-segregation in which Black ownership and control of economic institutions would be encouraged.

Appearing to be frustrated with the inability to make any major inroads toward eliminating segregation, Du Bois argued that desegregation was likely to take a long time to achieve. During the interim, instead of focusing all of its energies on demands for integration, the Black community would be better served by developing and relying on its own institutions.

Although it was not his intention, the editorial was perceived as acquiescing to continued segregation. The editorial set off a vigorous debate within the civil rights community. Years later, Roy Wilkins, who became executive director, said the editorials touched off an "uproar" at the NAACP's headquarters. To most observers, Du Bois seemed to be returning to the philosophy of Booker T. Washington, a view that Du Bois himself had rejected years earlier. Walter White, members of the Board, and other supporters of the NAACP were beside themselves with anger.

Du Bois had been allowed to operate the Crisis as an autonomous entity within the organizational framework of the NAACP. Editorial judgments concerning the journal's content were made by Du Bois without any interference from the Board or staff. For years, this arrangement had been satisfactory. By the early 1930s, however, the circulation of the Crisis had dropped from 100,000 issues per month to approximately 10,000. The publication was rapidly losing money. Du Bois attempted unsuccessfully to recruit Roy Wilkins as a business manager for the Crisis. But, Du Bois' reputation as a "prickly" personality persuaded Wilkins to decline the offer. White recruited individuals to write a reply. Ultimately, William Hastie, a prominent African American lawyer, authored a stinging reply to the segregation editorials.

After several meetings, the NAACP's Board adopted a resolution requiring editorials to reflect the organization's institutional views. In addition, all future editorials would need advance approval by the Board. This would have been a dramatic alteration of the editorial independence Du Bois had exercised since the founding of the *Crisis*. The Board's censure was more than he could take. In June of 1934, Du Bois tendered his resignation with a bitter letter to the Board.[3] With Du Bois' departure Walter White was left firmly in control. The organization would soon embark on a full-fledged litigation campaign.

In the mid-1930s, the NAACP's Board decided to hire a lawyer to serve full-time as the organization's counsel and lead the litigation campaign. It eventually settled on Charles Hamilton Houston for the position. At the time, he was the Dean of Howard University's law school. During his time there, he trained a generation of African American lawyers who would serve as soldiers in the battle for civil rights. Houston inspired his students with a sense of social mission, telling them, "A lawyer is either a social engineer or a parasite on society." Houston introduced a number of improvements to the law school, ending its part-time program and gaining accreditation from the American Association of Law schools.[4]

Houston was a native of Washington D.C., where his father was a lawyer. Houston attended Amherst College, where he graduated with honors in 1915. When America entered the First World War, Houston volunteered to serve in the military, where he was appointed as an officer. During the war, Houston decided to pursue a career in law after witnessing the mistreatment of African American soldiers. Houston enrolled in Harvard Law School, where he was elected to the prestigious Harvard Law Review.

After graduating with a Doctor of Laws degree in 1923 and studying at the University of Madrid in 1924, Houston was admitted to the District of Columbia bar and joined his father's law practice. He subsequently joined the faculty at Howard Law school.[5] Houston also served on the NAACP's legal steering committee, where he was an advisor to the organization. In 1935, Houston accepted the NAACP's offer to serve as in-house legal counsel. He moved to New York City and commenced his service with the organization.

By the 1930s, the separate-but-equal doctrine was firmly entrenched. Houston did not want to risk an affirmation of *Plessy* given the conservative legal climate. He devised instead an indirect approach; the "equalization strategy." When the plan was implemented, cases would be filed arguing that states operating segregated schools were in violation of the Fourteenth Amendment based on the substandard and demonstrably unequal facilities maintained for Black students. Houston calculated that if the equality aspect of the "separate-but-equal" doctrine was enforced, states would be compelled to make Black schools physically and otherwise equal to the white institutions. States would not be able to bear the resulting economic burden. Segregation would eventually collapse under its own weight.

Houston's first equalization case involved the University of Maryland's law school. Thurgood Marshall graduated first in the class of 1933 at Howard. During his years at Howard, Houston mentored Marshall and allowed him to assist in some trials. After graduation, Marshall returned to Baltimore and set up a practice representing mainly poor clients. Some groups in Baltimore, including the Alpha Phi Alpha fraternity, were organizing an effort to challenge the University of Maryland's whites only policy. Marshall contacted Houston and asked him if the NAACP could sponsor the case. Houston ultimately decided to represent the plaintiff, Donald Murray. Houston and Marshall tried the case together in Baltimore city court.[6]

Maryland' lawyers argued that the state satisfied its obligation under *Plessy* with the establishment of Prince Anne Academy a Black school on Maryland's Eastern Shore. It also pointed to a scholarship fund that the state had established for African American students who wished to attend graduate and professional schools in states that permitted Black students to matriculate. Houston examined the president of the University of Maryland to prove that the provisions made for Black students were not equal to those provided for whites.

Houston started with questions comparing the facilities and faculty at the University of Maryland to those at Princess Anne Academy. The president reluctantly admitted that the facilities at Princess Anne Academy were not equal to those at the University of Maryland. Also, there were no scholarship funds available for Murray to attend an out-of-state school. At the conclusion of the trial, the judge ruled from the bench in Houston and Marshall's favor and ordered the admission of Murray to the entering class in the fall. The win was affirmed later by the Maryland Court of Appeals.

The next equalization case challenged segregation by the University of Missouri. Sidney Redmond, a Harvard Law School graduate, practiced law in St. Louis, Missouri. Redmond was active in the St. Louis affiliate of the National Bar Association and had served as the president of the national organization. Redmond recommended that a case be filed on behalf of Lloyd Gaines, a graduate of Lincoln University in Jefferson City, Missouri. Gaines had a strong academic record at Lincoln. He was poised and confident.

Houston traveled to St. Louis, arriving a few days ahead of the trial. On July 10, 1935, Houston rose at 4:15 a.m. to prepare for the 120-mile drive to Columbia, Missouri. Boone County, where the law school was located, was during a drought. Several farmers were in the courthouse seeking assistance from the state agencies that were located there. Several students from Lincoln University were also present to observe the trial. By the time the trial was convened, the courtroom was packed.

Houston was assisted at the trial by Sidney Redmond and Henry Espy, Redmond's partner. Gaines" attorneys and the lawyers for Missouri sat at the same table during the trial, in an arrangement that Houston noted as being a bit odd. Also, the restrooms in the courthouse were not segregated. As the trial proceeded, Houston noted that the disposition of the judge was not receptive. He concluded that an appeal would be needed. The case was appealed to the Missouri Supreme Court. As Gaines" lawyer noted there was no law requiring segregation. The Court held that there was a clear intention by the legislature to separate the white and Negro races for the purpose of higher education.

Lincoln Institute was established in 1866 in Jefferson City to provide college-level training for African Americans, but no provisions were made for graduate or professional training. Missouri, like other Southern states, had established an out-of-state scholarship for Black students to attend graduate and professional school. This arrangement, the Court found, satisfied Missouri's obligation to provide substantially equal educational arrangements for Black and white students. Segregation was upheld. In one concession, the Court also ruled that the funds provided by the out-of-state scholarships should be raised to cover the full cost of attending those schools.

The case was appealed to the Supreme Court. The University's lawyers argued that Gaines should have applied to the Curators of Lincoln University to establish a Black law school and that they would have been obligated to do so. The Supreme Court rejected this argument, stating that Missouri had made no provisions for legal training for Black students. The Court found that the real question was what provisions Missouri made for Black students. No such arrangements had been made. The Court found that out-of-state scholarships were not adequate. The right to equal protection is a "personal one" that had to be provided for Black students within the confines of Missouri.[7]

Gaines was an important victory for this NAACP. A decision by the Supreme Court would be binding on other cases that were brought in the future against other states. As a result of the court case, the Missouri General Assembly passed a bill that provided $275,000 for the creation and establishment of a law school for African Americans, the Lincoln University School of Law, which opened its doors on September 20, 1939. By 1954, the number of law students had decreased to twelve. The law school ceased operation because its expenses constituted a drain on the university's meager resources.

One of the strangest stories of major civil rights cases involved the final disposition of the *Gaines* case. After the cases were remanded to the trial court, the University scheduled a deposition for Gaines. After repeated efforts to contact him, it became apparent that he had disappeared. He was last seen in the Alpha Phi Alpha fraternity house in Chicago but was never seen again. Various theories exist as to what happened to Gaines, but all that is actually known is that he was never heard from again.[8]

In 1941 the Second World War began. From the early to the mid-1940s, the NAACP was active on several fronts. One important activity involved teacher salary cases. Throughout the South, segregated schools were staffed by African American teachers who were paid considerably less than their white counterparts. A series of suits were filed in various southern jurisdictions and were eventually won at the appellate and Supreme Court levels.[9] These victories contributed to the expansion of the NAACP's membership rolls. Black teachers were the educated and influential backbones of the communities where they were located.

The NAACP also fought discrimination in the Armed Forces. It represented defendants in criminal cases. Discrimination in housing was another area in which the organization was active. Several housing cases were brought by the NAACP itself or by cooperating attorneys in various locations. The problem in the North and the South involved restrictive covenants which limited the occupancy of neighborhoods to whites. The NAACP had successfully challenged local ordinances which restricted neighborhood occupancy in *Buchanan v. Warley*.[10] The Court held the ordinances violated the Fourteenth Amendment. After that decision, the real estate industry developed racially restrictive covenants as a means of excluding African Americans from white neighborhoods.

These were private agreements that were not subject to the Fourteenth Amendment. The Great Migration was in high gear in the 1930s and 1940s. African Americans were moving into northern and midwestern cities in large numbers. By the 1940s, most American cities were covered with race restrictive covenants. These contributed to a severe housing shortage for African American families. African Americans were crowded into older neighborhoods in or near the center of cities. In the mid-1940s, the NAACP coordinated a legal strategy to challenge the covenants. Meetings were held at which the NAACP's lawyers discussed strategies for attacking the covenants.

Ultimately, cases reached the Supreme Court. One was from St. Louis, Missouri. Another arose in Detroit, Michigan, and the other case involved the District of Columbia. In an earlier case, *Corrigan v. Buckley*, the Court of Appeals for the District of Columbia held that the covenants were private and not subject to the Equal Protection Clause of the Fourteenth Amendment. The Supreme Court declined an appeal. The successful strategy in the Supreme Court cases was an argument that while the covenants themselves were private, the judicial enforcement of covenants was state action prohibited by the Fourteenth Amendment *Shelley v. Kraemer; McGhee v. Sipes*, 334 US 1 (1948); *Hurd v. Hodge*, 334 US 24 (1948).[11]

After the close of the Second World War, the NAACP returned its attention to higher education. There were many African Americans who wanted to use the G.I. Bill to fund their college careers. In 1946, Thurgood Marshall filed a suit against the University of Oklahoma using the equalization strategy. Marshall argued that Oklahoma was obligated to provide graduate and professional training for African American students, but no such provisions had been made. In a brief, *per curiam*, opinion the Supreme Court held in 1948 that Oklahoma was obligated to make provisions for legal education for African American students. The State of Oklahoma responded by renting a few rooms in the state capital and hiring a couple of law professors to serve as the faculty. Marshall petitioned the Supreme Court, objecting to this response. The Supreme Court concluded that Oklahoma had satisfied its obligation to provide legal training for African American students.[12]

While the Oklahoma case was pending, the NAACP filed an identical lawsuit, *Sweatt v. Painter*, against the state of Texas. It responded by renting a few rooms in Houston and hiring two Black lawyers to serve as faculty for the newly established branch of Prairie View University, the school previously established to serve Black students. At a status hearing convened a few months later, the trial court found that the facilities in Houston were substantially equal to the provisions made for white students at Texas' main campus. [13]

While the appeal was pending, Texas took steps to establish a new law school for Black students. The legislature allocated $100,000 for the construction of the institution. While the Texas case was pending, another case was filed against the University of Oklahoma. George McLaurin applied to the Graduate School of Education at the University of Oklahoma. After his application was denied, the NAACP filed a suit on his behalf.[14] *Sweatt* and *McLaurin* reached the Supreme Court at the same time. McLaurin was argued on April 3 and 4, and Sweatt on April 4. The decisions in both cases were issued on April 5.

The Court declined the NAACP's request to consider whether *Plessy v. Ferguson* should be reversed, but the opinions both cases came close to acknowledging the inherent equities of state-sponsored segregation. In *Sweatt*, the court found that the facilities available at the newly established law school were not equal in quantity or quality to those available at the law school in Austin. A law school consists of more than bricks and mortar. Intangible features such as the reputation of the school and faculty and the interactions of students could not be replicated at a separate facility. Oklahoma required McLaurin to sit at a separate table in the library, a separate table at lunch, and a roped-off corner in the classroom. These arrangements, the Court found, stigmatized and handicapped McLaurin in his efforts to study.

In 1950, the NAACP held another conference for the lawyers and consultants who were working on desegregation cases. During that meeting, the conferees adopted the resolution that in all future cases, relief would be aimed at obtaining education on a non-segregated basis. The equalization had finally evolved into a direct attack on segregation policy. At about the same time, the NAACP decided to challenge segregation in secondary and primary school cases.

Brown v. Board of Education consisted of six cases filed in five separate jurisdictions. The *Brown* case arose in Topeka, Kansas. Companion cases were filed in South Carolina, Delaware, Virginia, and the District of Columbia.[15] All of the cases involved challenges to segregation at the elementary school level. The plaintiffs were represented by lawyers associated with the NAACP. In South Carolina, the judge hearing the case indicated during a pretrial hearing that he did not believe that segregation as a *per se* violation of the Constitution had been raised in the pleadings. He dismissed the case without prejudice and suggested that the pleadings be amended and the case be brought before a three-judge district court (from which direct appeals to the Supreme Court were allowed). When the case was refiled, the direct challenge to segregation was launched.

One of the keys to the direct challenge cases involved expert testimony to establish the severe psychological harm that segregation inflicted on Black children and its impact on the educational process. There were several experts who aided the NAACP in school desegregation cases, but one stands out for the simple but compelling test he devised to demonstrate the disabling effects of discrimination. In 1951, Kenneth Clark was a psychologist and assistant professor at City College of New York. Clark and his wife Mamie had developed a series of studies concerning the effects of segregation on young children.[16] The Clarks asked a series of questions to children who were aged three to seven. The questions included:

1. give me the dog you like to play with;
2. give me the doll that is a nice doll;
3. give me the doll that looks bad and;
4. give me the doll that is a nice color.

The students consistently showed a decided preference for the white dolls. The Clarks also developed a coloring test in which Black children were given a set of crayons and a number of objects to color. Students were provided with outline drawings. Students with dark complexions did not select an accurate color when interviewers asked them to select a color that resembled them. The Clarks concluded their studies demonstrated self-rejection as one of the effects of racism on children in the early stages of their development.

Thurgood Marshall represented the South Carolina plaintiffs in *Briggs v. Elliot*. The plaintiffs, who were the parents of African American students, originally wanted the Clarendon County school board to provide a school bus for their children. They were persuaded by Marshall to pursue a direct challenge to segregation itself. The proof in the case consisted of two components. One aspect challenged the disparities in the facilities that were provided to Black and white students. The schools for Black students were physically and otherwise grossly inferior to the white schools. The NAACP lawyers also introduced expert testimony which showed the psychological impact of segregation on African American students. At the start of the trial, the Carolina's lawyers admitted that the facilities for Black students were inferior to those provided for whites. They stated that taxes were being levied to equalize the Black and white schools. Marshall did not accept the state's proposal. The trial court ruled against the NAACP.

Proof in the other cases proceeds along the same lines. In Virginia, a group of students organized a protest against the disparities between Black and white schools. Sixteen-year-old Barbara Johns led a student strike against inadequate facilities at the grossly overcrowded Moton High School in Farmville. When the students sought the assistance of the NAACP, the local cooperating lawyers, pottswood Robinson and Oliver Hill, agreed to take the case only if the students agreed to a direct challenge to segregation. In *Davis v. Prince Edward County, Virginia*, the lawyers introduced evidence concerning the physical disparities in the schools and expert testimony which indicated the stigmatic and psychological injuries. The trial court ruled against the NAACP's lawyers.

In the Topeka, Kansas case Robert Carter, an NAACP staff attorney, represented Oliver Brown and the other plaintiffs. They were a group of parents who objected to traveling past a well-appointed white high school to a less well-kept facility for Black students. The physical disparities in Topeka were not as gross as they were in other localities. Carter emphasized expert testimony which focused on the psychological effects of segregation on young Black children. When the trial court decided the case, it made a number of factual findings agreeing with the disparities in the Black and white schools but concluded that it lacked the authority to overrule *Plessy*.

The District of Columbia case began on September 11, 1950. Gardner Bishop and the Consolidated Parents Group attempted to get eleven African American students admitted to the all-white John Philip Sousa Junior High. The school's principal refused. A suit was filed with James Nabit representing the plaintiffs. Unlike the other desegregation cases, the District of Columbia is not a state to which the Fourteenth Amendment applies. The Supreme Court relied instead on the Due Process Clause of the Fifth Amendment. It stated considering the decision in *Brown* that segregation was prohibited by the Constitution; it would have been unthinkable for the Constitution to impose a lesser duty on the Federal Government.

Two cases were filed in Delaware: *Bulah v. Gephardt* and *Belton v. Gelbart*. Sarah Beulah was a white woman who adopted a Black child. She lived in Hockessin, Delaware, which is a few miles from Wilmington. She was upset because she was forced to drive past a well-appointed school for white children to a dilapidated, one-room school for Blacks. The other case involved a school in Claymont, Delaware, which is just a few miles north of Wilmington. Claymont had a modern, well-equipped school for white students. Black students had to travel to Wilmington to attend Howard High School, which was the only high school for Black students. The facilities in Claymont were modern and well-equipped. The teachers were well-qualified. The plaintiffs in both cases were represented by Louis Redding and Jack Greenberg. At the trials in both cases, the evidence consisted of comparisons of the physical facilities for Black and white students' along with expert testimony on the impact of segregation on Black students' educational progress.

The cases were heard by Chancellor Collins Seitz. He had presided over a case presented by Louis Reading which desegregated the University of Delaware in 1950. As he had in the University of Delaware case, Seitz visited the locations of the schools and made an item-by-item comparison. The inventory was stated in the court's opinion. Seitz found that the facilities were not equal as *Plessy v. Ferguson* required. As a result, he ordered the admission of the Black students to the white schools in Claymont and Hockessin. These were the only cases that the NAACP lawyers won at the trial court level.

All of the cases were appealed and consolidated in the Supreme Court. The cases were set down for argument in 1952. The arguments were presented, but an order was issued setting the cases down for re-argument in 1953. The court issued a series of questions to be answered, such as the original intent of the Fourteenth Amendment and the manner in which a decision would be implemented if the NAACP lawyers prevailed. A decision in the cases was issued on May 17, 1954. The court held that segregation in public education violated the Equal Protection Clause of the Fourteenth Amendment. The cases were set down for yet another argument on the question of the implementation of the Court's desegregation decree. A hearing was held in 1955, and the Court issued an order in which the cases were remanded to the trial courts for the implementation of the decree with "all deliberate speed."[17]

In a Detroit, Michigan, case, the NAACP argued that school desegregation could not succeed without including the suburban districts in the desegregation plan based on urban-suburban demographic patterns. The Supreme Court held that suburban school districts could not be required to participate in court-ordered desegregation plans unless it could be proven that their actions contributed to segregation in the jurisdiction in which the case arose. After Milliken, suburban school districts were effectively protected from school desegregation efforts. School desegregation proceeded within school districts, relying heavily on bussing to achieve racial balance

Over the next several years, school desegregation proceeded slowly with courts relying heavily on bussing to achieve racial balance. During the same period, residential segregation in urban areas increased substantially despite the anti-discrimination requirements of the Fair Housing Act of 1968.

In the early 1990s, the Supreme Court's desegregation jurisprudence took a dramatic shift with the decisions in *Board of Education of Oklahoma City v. Dowell*, *Freeman v. Pitts*, and *Missouri v. Jenkins*. The Court held that a determination of unitary status could be made when a trial court found that the school board had complied in "good faith" with the desegregation decree since it was entered, and the vestiges of past discrimination had been eliminated to the "extent practicable *Dowell* and *Freeman* effectively abandoned the *Green* standard, which imposed an affirmative duty to eliminate all vestiges of segregation 'root and branch.'"

This was affirmed in *Jenkins*. The majority stated that the test for determining unitary status was "whether the [school district] ha[s] complied in good faith with the desegregation decree since it was entered, and whether the vestiges of past discrimination ha[ve] been eliminated to the extent practicable."

Notes

1 Library of Congress NAACP: A Century in the Fight for Freedom: The Great Depression.

2 Nathan R. Margold, *Preliminary Report to the Joint Committee Supervising the Expenditure of the 1930 Appropriation by the American Fund for Public Service* (1931). Typescript. Page 2—Page 3—Page 4—Page 5—Page 6—Page 7—Page 8. NAACP Records, Manuscript Division, Library of Congress (070.00.00) Courtesy of the NAACP.

3 Letter from W. E. B. Du Bois to NAACP Board of Directors, Jun. 26, 1934.https://credo.library.umass.edu/view/full/mums312-b071-i296.

4 Genna Rae McNeil, *Groundwork: Charles Hamilton Houston and the Struggle for Civil Rights* (Philadelphia: University of Pennsylvania Press, 1983). For examinations of the history and circumstances surrounding the NAACP's legal campaign against school segregation, see e.g., Robert J. Cottrol, Raymond Diamond and Leland Ware, *Brown v. Board of Education: Caste, Culture and the Constitution* (University Press of Kansas, 2003); Michael Davis and Hunter R. Clark, *Thurgood Marshall: Warrior at the Bar, Rebel on the Bench* (Carol Publishing Corporation, 1992); Jack Greenberg, *Crusaders in the Courts: How a*

Dedicated Band of Lawyers Fought for the Civil Rights Revolution (Basic Books, 1994); Peter H. Irons, *Jim Crow's Children: The Broken Promise of the Brown Decision* (Penguin Books, 2002); Richard Kluger, *Simple Justice: The History of Brown v. Board of Education and Black America's Struggle for Equality* (Vintage Books, 1975); James T. Patterson, *Brown v. Board of Education: A Civil Rights Milestone and Its Troubled Legacy* (Oxford University Press, 2001); Mark V. Tushnet, *Making Civil Rights Law: Thurgood Marshall and the Supreme Court 1936–1961* (Oxford University Press, 1994); Mark V. Tushnet, *The NAACP's Legal Strategy against Segregated Education, 1925–1950* (University of North Carolina Press, 1987). Juan Williams, *Thurgood Marshall: American Revolutionary* (Three Rivers Press, 1998); Patricia Sullivan, *Lift Every Voice: The NAACP and the Making of the Civil Rights Movement* (The New Press, 2009); Robert L. Carter, *A Matter of Law: A Memoir* (The New Press, 2005).

5 NAACP. explained/civil-rights-leaders/charles-hamilton-houston.

6 *Murray v. Pierson* 169 Md. 478, 182 A. 590 (1936).

7 *Missouri ex rel. Gaines v. Canada*, 305 US 337 (1938).

8 Rawn James, *Root And Branch: Charles Hamilton Houston, Thurgood Marshall, And the Struggle to End Segregation* (2010).

9 John A. Kirk, *The NAACP Campaign for Teachers' Salary Equalization: African American Women Educators and The Early Civil Rights Struggle*, 94(4) JAAH 529–52 (2009).

10 *Buchanan v. Warley*, 245 US 60 (1917).

11 Leland Ware, *Invisible Walls: An Examination of the Legal Strategy of the Restrictive Covenant Cases,* 67 Washington U. L. Quarterly (1989).

12 *Sipuel v. Board of Regents of the University of Oklahoma*, 332 US 631 (1948).

13 *Sweatt v. Painter*, 339 US 629 (1950).

14 *McLaurin v. Oklahoma State Regents*, 339 US 637 (1950).

15 In October 1952, the Court consolidated *Brown* with three other class-action school-segregation lawsuits filed by the NAACP: *Briggs* v. *Elliott* (1951) in South Carolina, *Davis* v. *County School Board of Prince Edward County* (1952) in Virginia, and *Gebhart* v. *Belton* (1952) in Delaware; a fifth case was filed independently in the District of Columbia, *Bolling* v. *Sharpe* (1951).

16 The coloring test was an experiment that was involved in the *Brown* decision. Mamie and Kenneth conducted an experiment to investigate the development of racial identity in African American children and examine how a Black child's color and influenced "their judgment about themselves" and their "self-esteem."

17 *Brown v. Board of Education of Topeka*, 349 US 294 (1955).

4

Student Disparities

Teachers and other school officials in districts across the nation are exercising their discretion in ways that treat African American students differently and less favorably than similarly situated white students. Academic studies produced over the past 30 years have consistently found racial disparities in the administration of discipline. Discipline is imposed more frequently and with heavier penalties on African American students than white students who engage in the same conduct.

Researchers also found that the large and persistent overrepresentation of African American students in misconduct referrals, suspensions, and other forms of discipline was not attributable to racial differences in classroom conduct. When researchers controlled for differences in behavior, student demeanor, or personality traits (concentration, extroversion, closeness with teacher), grades, and other factors, African American students were still far more likely to be disciplined than white students.

Until recently, the academic research focused on specific geographic regions within the nation. However, the US Department of Education's Office for Civil Rights' 2014 report on school discipline collected data on a nationwide basis and found glaring racial disparities in the imposition of discipline. This meant the depth and scope of the problem were much greater than previously known. An entire generation of African American students are being denied access to equal educational opportunities.

Although the racial disparities have been documented, the underlying causes have not been explored. Over the last three decades, a substantial body of research in cognitive psychology and other disciplines has confirmed that the causes of discriminatory actions often operate at an unconscious level without the perpetrator's awareness of the source. Explicit expressions of racial attitudes have become less frequent, but people often harbor more racially prejudiced views than they consciously realize. Implicit biases are supplanting explicit racism, but they have the same deleterious effects. This chapter analyzes the influence of implicit bias on student discipline. More than 60 years after *Brown v. Board of Education*[1] African American students are being denied equal access to educational opportunities in the nation's public schools.

The Department of Education's Discipline Data

The US Department of Education's Office for Civil Rights (OCR) released a report on school discipline that found glaring racial disparities in the imposition of discipline on a nationwide basis.[2] The report, a compilation of disciplinary reports for 16,500 school districts, which are collectively responsible for 97,000 schools with 49 million students, revealed pervasive racial disparities across localities, age groups, and disability statuses.

The data disclosed disparities in out-of-school suspensions beginning at the earliest stages of educational development. In the 2011–2012 school year, African American children accounted for 18 percent of preschool enrollment and 48 percent of preschoolers who were given more than one out-of-school suspension. By contrast, of the 43 percent of white preschoolers, 26 percent were given more than one out-of-school suspension. The proportion of Black preschoolers receiving one or more out-of-school suspensions exceeded all other racial/ethnic groups in seventeen states. In fourteen of these states, at least half of all preschoolers suspended out-of-school were African American. In Georgia, 1,657 Black preschoolers received at least one out-of-school suspension, of a total of 1,949 suspensions issued in the school year; African Americans accounted for 178 of the 186 preschoolers suspended at least once in the District of Columbia; and, in Wisconsin, fifty-two Black preschoolers were suspended compared to thirteen white preschoolers.

Collectively, Black students were suspended and expelled at a rate three times greater than their white counterparts. Although two-thirds of suspensions were given to boys, 12 percent or 3.7 million suspensions were given to African American girls, the highest proportion of any female racial or ethnic group. Concerning suspensions and expulsions, Black students represent 16 percent of the student population and approximately 32 to 42 percent of students suspended or expelled from their schools. White students, who made up slightly over half of the students enrolled in school, account for about 31 to 40 percent of students who are suspended or expelled. Disciplinary disparities were also present in other forms of punishment. In the same period, 27 percent of Black students were referred to law enforcement officials, and 31 percent were involved in school-related arrests. White students represented 41 percent of law enforcement referrals and 39 percent of arrests. In all types of punishment, the proportion of African American students punished was at least ten percentage points higher than their proportion in the general student population.

Corporal Punishment

Black students constituted 34.6 percent of students who received corporal punishment in the 2011–12 school year, although they made up only 16 percent of the student population. This indicates that their representation among the corporally punished was eighteen percentage points higher than their representation in the general school population. In the states of Georgia, Louisiana, Maine, Missouri, Ohio, Pennsylvania, and Rhode Island, African American students' share of corporal punishment was at least ten percentage points higher than their share of the student population. In these same states, the percentage of white students receiving corporal punishment was seven to thirty-seven percentage points lower than their proportion in the student population.

Suspensions

At the national level, the proportion of in-school suspensions given to Black students was fifteen percentage points higher than their overall proportion of the student population. The proportion of white students with in-school suspensions was 10 percent less than their proportion in the student population.

Within all of the twenty-four states where Black students were overrepresented by more than ten percentage points, white students were underrepresented by at least six percentage points.

Over 1.2 million African American students were suspended out-of-school at least once while 1.08 million white students received this punishment. Although 51 percent of all public students were white in the 2011–12 academic year, they constituted only 34 percent of those suspended out-of-school. African American students were suspended at a higher proportion than their general enrollment in every state. On average, Black students were overrepresented in out-of-school suspensions by twenty-two percentage points. In thirty-three states and the District of Columbia, the proportion of African American students suspended from school was at least ten percentage points higher than their representation in student enrollment. In Georgia, Louisiana, Maryland, and Mississippi, twice as many Black students were suspended compared to white students. In Delaware, three times more African American students were suspended out-of-school than their white counterparts.

In the period studied, 604,181 African American students were suspended from school multiple times while 444,670 white students received the same punishment. Proportionally, Black students accounted for 43 percent of those sanctioned. This was 27 percent higher than their proportion in the general population. The proportion of white students with more than one out-of-school suspension was 20 percent less than their proportion in the school population. In thirty-one states and the District of Columbia, African American students constituted at least a 10 percent greater proportion of students receiving multiple suspensions than their proportion in the student population. white students were underrepresented by anywhere from 3 to 38 percent in these same states.

Expulsions, Referrals, and Arrests

In the expulsion category, Black students were overrepresented by twenty percentage points while white students were underrepresented by 15 percent. Of the 1,476 students expelled in Maryland, 1,156 were African American. African American students accounted for 55 percent of the expulsions in New

Jersey although they constituted only 16 percent of all the state's public school students. In Tennessee, where white students constitute 68 percent of the student population, only 26 percent were expelled. 70 percent of expulsions were given to African American students, who represent 23 percent of public school enrollment.

At the national level, the proportion of Black students referred to law enforcement and arrested in school-related incidents exceeded their proportion in enrollment by 11 percent and 14 percent respectively. African American students were overrepresented in law enforcement referrals by at least ten percentage points in twenty states, as well as the District of Columbia. School-related arrests of Black students exceeded their enrollment proportions by more than 10 percent in twenty-six states. White students were underrepresented by at least 5 percent in relation to their enrollment proportions in forty states.

Zero Tolerance Policies

African American students' proportion in zero tolerance expulsions was 7 percent higher than their enrollment proportions. White students' expulsions were 12 percent less than their enrollment proportions. Black students' zero tolerance expulsions in Connecticut were more than twice their proportion in enrollment. Oklahoma's Black students accounted for 9 percent of enrollment and 38 percent of expulsions in this category. Massachusetts' Black students accounted for 8 percent of the public school population and 20 percent of expulsions under zero tolerance.

Unconscious Discrimination

In the case of student discipline, minority students suffer injuries caused by teachers treating them differently and less favorably than similarly situated white students. Over the last three decades, a substantial body of empirical and theoretical work across a range of academic disciplines has determined that the causes of discriminatory actions often operate at an unconscious level without the individual's awareness of the source. Building on well-established scientific methods and principles from the field of cognitive psychology, researchers have provided a solid empirical foundation for understanding implicit bias. The studies have been replicated in hundreds of peer-reviewed articles.[3] They demonstrate that individuals can possess attitudes, stereotypes, and prejudices in the absence of awareness, intention, or deliberation. Decades of research on automatic, associative links in memory among words and concepts that are related to one another led to the discovery that stereotyping and prejudice might also operate implicitly. By the early 1980s, a scientific consensus emerged regarding the ubiquity of unconscious and automatic cognition.

The first demonstrations of implicit stereotyping and prejudice were extensions of the well-established cognitive principle that knowledge is organized in memory in the form of associations that are derived from personal experiences as well as normative procedures and rules. The discovery of implicit prejudice evolved from nearly a century's worth of research on perception, memory, and learning. The phenomenon of implicit bias was incorporated into existing principles of human information processing. It fits the current consensus in brain and behavioral sciences that a substantial amount of cognition occurs automatically, effortlessly, and outside of an individual's conscious awareness of the source.

Some of the earliest experiments were conducted by Professors Dovidio and Gaertner, who used the term "aversive racism" to describe the conduct of individuals who support policies that promote racial equality and regard themselves as not prejudiced but act in ways that disadvantage minorities.[4] Aversive racists, they explained, often experience feelings of *uneasiness or fear* in the presence of African Americans. Their negative attitudes toward minorities are usually unacknowledged.[5] Their attitudes are rooted in cognitive, motivational, and socio-cultural forces that affect many white Americans.

Aversive racists typically do not discriminate against African Americans when it would be obvious to others and themselves, but they are likely to engage in such behavior when there are race-neutral justifications for their actions.[6] In one frequently cited study concerning the provision of emergency assistance, white bystanders were as likely to help a Black victim as a white victim when they were the only witness to an emergency and their personal responsibility was clear. In circumstances in which there were other witnesses to the emergency, they would justify not helping on the belief that someone else would intervene. In this situation, whites helped the Black victim half as often as they helped the white victim. Racial bias was expressed in a way that could be justified by a race neutral reason.[7]

Legal scholars began to study this phenomenon in the late 1980s, which they labeled "unconscious discrimination." In one of the seminal articles, Professor Charles Lawrence employed social cognition and Freudian theories in his critique of the limitations of antidiscrimination law. In *The Id, the Ego and Equal Protection Reckoning with Unconscious Racism*, Professor Lawrence relied on Freudian psychology to explain that our culture transmits various beliefs and preferences that are not experienced as explicit lessons.[8] Instead, they are part of individuals' rational ordering of their perceptions of the world. These individuals are not aware of how the ubiquitous presence of cultural stereotypes influences their perception that Blacks are lazy or unintelligent. Young children may not be told that Blacks are inferior, they learn that lesson through observing the behavior of others. Professor Frances Aboud, who conducted research on prejudice in young children, found that stereotypes develop between the ages of three and five and are retained in the unconscious psyche as children mature into adulthood.[9]

In a 1995 article, *The Content of Our Categories*,[10] Professor Linda Krieger explained that much of the discrimination that occurs now is not the result of conscious animus. Krieger relied on social cognition theory to explain that decision-making relies on "categorization," which is a fundamental part of the process of human cognition. Categorization simplifies the task of processing and retaining information. It allows individuals to identify objects and make predictions about future events. Categorization operates automatically at an unconscious level. Individuals perceive, categorize, and evaluate information differently depending on the ways in which information is presented and the context in which it is received. The process occurs in milliseconds without the individual experiencing a conscious awareness that it is happening.

The danger of categorization is that it can cause judgment errors that bias decision-making. Categorization can make it difficult for an observer to recognize a person's individual characteristics. When an individual is seen as a member of a social group, perceptions about that group's characteristics and behavior influence judgments made about them. Stereotypes can be so deeply internalized that they persist even in the face of information that directly contradicts the stereotype.[11]

Krieger and Fiske explained that subtle forms of intergroup bias can affect decision-making long before any decision is made. These biases can distort the perceptual data set on which decisions are premised. Operating outside of the decision maker's awareness, stereotypes can powerfully influence the way information about the stereotyped target is processed. They can shape the interpretation of incoming information and influence the manner in which that information is encoded into and stored in memory. Decision makers can act on the basis of a person's race and/or sex while subjectively believing they are acting on the basis of a legitimate, nondiscriminatory reason.[12]

A widely used experiment demonstrates how unconscious discrimination operates. The IAT measures automatic association response times between representations for race, gender, and age, and other classifications of positive and negative characteristics.[13] To measure racial associations, test takers' preferences are measured by their response times in pairing positive words or negative words with depictions of alternating white and Black faces. Quicker response times to pairing Black faces with negative words and white faces with positive words indicate an implicit preference for a Black or white face with a negative or positive word.[14]

The test is premised on the conclusion that it takes participants longer to associate words and faces that the test takers consider incompatible. The test developers determined that the time differential could be quantified to provide an objective assessment of a test taker's unconscious attitudes. Using the IAT, researchers have documented a marked preference for whites among test takers of different races who consciously believed that their views about race were neutral. The test results indicate that the test taker's attitudes about race were influenced by unconscious bias.[15] In a recent study, the authors analyzed 122 research reports to establish the validity and efficacy of implicit association tests. They found that the tests are highly effective in measuring implicit bias.[16]

In *Advocacy Against the Stereotype: Lessons From Cognitive Social Psychology*, Professor Gary Blasi surveyed experiments, theories, and models in cognitive social psychology and social neuroscience that explain how unconscious stereotypes function in the human mind. The extensive body of research that Blasi cataloged showed that individuals behave in ways that demonstrate that they are heavily influenced by stereotypes, including those that they consciously disavow.

A thorough and exhaustive review of the social science literature authored by John T. Jost and others was published in 2009. After reviewing hundreds of studies conducted over more than three decades, the authors concluded that "the existence of implicit bias is beyond a reasonable doubt."

The Perpetuation of African American Stereotypes

Unconscious stereotypes about African American students have a significant influence on how their conduct is evaluated by teachers. Stereotyping involves the creation of a mental image of a typical member of a particular category. Individuals are perceived as undifferentiated members of a group, lacking any significant differences from other individuals within the group. Common traits are assigned to the entire group. When a particular behavior by a group member is observed, the viewer evaluates the behavior through the lens of the stereotype. This causes the observer to conclude that the conduct has empirically confirmed their stereotyped belief about the group.

Stereotypes and the ideology of Black inferiority are deeply embedded in American culture. Some of the best-selling popular literature of the late nineteenth and early twentieth century perpetuated negative stereotypes. Thomas Dixon Jr., one of the popular authors of the period, published a number of novels which depicted the Reconstruction Era. One of these, *The Clansman: A Historical Romance of the Ku Klux Klan*[17], glorified the activities of the Klan and portrayed it as a protector of the Southern way of life. Charles Carroll's *"Negro a Beast" or "In the Image of God"*[18] was patterned along the same lines. African American stereotypes became a popular vehicle for entertainment. Beginning in the early nineteenth century, white performers darkened their faces with burnt cork, painted exaggerated white mouths, donned woolly wigs, and took to the stage.

The common theme in all these shows was jokes highlighting laziness, ignorance, and other negative traits using crude versions of the Black dialect. One of the Black-faced characters created in the mid-nineteenth century was Jim Crow, whose name became synonymous with the system of segregation. During the closing years of the nineteenth century, minstrel shows featuring white performers in blackface were a popular mainstay of traveling shows and vaudeville productions.[19] Later, African American entertainers performed in minstrel shows.[20]

With the advent of motion pictures in the early twentieth century, negative depictions of African Americans moved from the stage to the screen. African American stereotypes were prominently featured in films for most of the twentieth century. In *Toms, Coons, Mulattoes, Mammies, and Bucks*[21] Donald Bogle identified the principal stereotypes depicted in films. These included "Toms," "Coons," "Mammies," "Mulattoes," and "Bucks." The "Toms" were usually humiliated, harassed, flogged, and insulted. The name Tom was derived from the character in Harriet Beecher Stowe's nineteenth century best-seller, *Uncle Tom's Cabin*. In films, "Toms" were always loyal, never turning against their white masters or employers.[22] "Toms" were always depicted as submissive, selfless, and kind—traits that endeared them to white audiences.

"Coons" were unreliable, irresponsible, lazy, and dishonest. They were frequently depicted eating watermelons, stealing chickens, or shooting craps while speaking grammatically incorrect English.[23] The "Mammy" was similar to the "Coon," except for her outspokenness and independence. She was usually depicted as overweight and cantankerous.[24] The "Tragic Mulatto" was a fair-skinned Black (usually female) attempting to pass for white.[25] The "Mulatto" was a tragic but sympathetic character whose fate would have been better had she not been confused by a divided racial heritage. The "Black Buck" was a large, brutal, fearsome, and oversexed male.[26]

D.W. Griffith's 1915 *Birth of a Nation* depicted Reconstruction in the Jim Crow South and contributed to the image of the "Black Buck" stereotype of men who lusted after innocent white women. It also glorified and romanticized the Ku Klux Klan. The film was based on Thomas Dixon's *The Clansman* and *The Leopard's Spots*. The film's message was that Blacks could not be integrated into white society as equals. The Klan's violent actions were necessary to overthrow the corrupt local governments of the Reconstruction Era South. President Woodrow Wilson, who was a friend of Thomas Dixon, screened *Birth of a Nation* in the White House. After viewing the film, Wilson said, "[i]t is like writing history with lightning."[27] For many years, it was the top-grossing film and is still viewed as a historic advance in cinematography.

In the 1939 film *Gone with the Wind*, the "Mammy" character in this film is actually called Mammy. *Gone with the Wind's* Mammy was a surrogate mother to her master's white children. The "Mammy" character was depicted as loving her white children more than her own. The character was happy, humorous, and steadfast as the world crumbled around Scarlett O'Hara's family during the Civil War.

Song of the South[28] was a Walt Disney film adaptation of African American folk tales transcribed in the late nineteenth century by Joel Chandler Harris in Uncle Remus tales.[29] The film, which was released in 1946, presented a romanticized version of the South with no references to racial problems in the post-Civil War era. The African American characters were portrayed as being happy and content in their subservient roles. Groups of African American field workers sang happily as they returned home each day from work. The Uncle Remus character fit Bogle's "Tom" model, and the film was replete with other demeaning stereotypes. *Song of the South* was popular and successful, but several years later, it was withdrawn from distribution after repeated protests by civil rights groups.

Stereotyped representations of African Americans were a staple of films, cartoons, and novels well into the 1960s. They reflected whites' perceptions of Blacks and institutionalized stereotypes in American popular culture. Amos and Andy was one of the most popular radio programs in the 1930s. One of the principal characters, Kingfish, was a dishonest schemer who entertained audiences with his failed schemes and mangled grammar. Andy was slightly dim-witted and gullible to Kingfish's schemes. Lightnin' was a slow moving, slow talking janitor. Andy was portrayed as a philosophical taxi driver. Kingfish fit Bogle's "Coon" paradigm. The female character, Sapphire, was Kingfish's loud and abrasive wife, who was a variation on the "Mammy" theme. The program was broadcast on radio in the 1930s and 1940s. It was a popular television program in the 1950s.[30]

African American stereotypes were featured in product advertisements. Aunt Jemima promoted pancake mixes, Uncle Ben sold rice, and Uncle Rastus was the Cream of Wheat chef. Aunt Jemima's character was based on a real woman, Nancy Green; her image is still the icon for pancake mixes. She is an example of the "Mammy" image. Rastus, the Cream of Wheat chef, was derived from a photograph of a Black Chicago waiter, whose name is unknown. The product is still marketed with that image. Uncle Ben is based on a photograph of Chicago maitre d', Frank Brown, a friend of the product's developers. Both characters are representations of a smiling, kindly "Tom" character.[31]

African American stereotypes were a staple in consumer products. They were represented in dolls, toys, children's books, salt and pepper shakers, packaged food, and many other household items. In popular periodicals such as *Harper's Weekly*, *The Saturday Evening Post*, and *The Atlantic Monthly*, African Americans were routinely portrayed as buffoons, criminals, or rapists.[32] The negative stereotypes of African Americans were ubiquitous and taken for granted as accurate portrayals. Newspapers, books, radio programs, and films reinforced negative stereotypes on a daily basis. Stereotypes rooted in our national consciousness for centuries, including the dangerous Black male persist into today.

Young African American Male Stereotypes

Black males experience the highest levels of discipline in schools. Young, African American males have long been stereotyped as violent, drug-involved criminals.[33] They are seen as angry, withdrawn, crude, disrespectful, provocative, unfeeling thugs.[34] One study showed that Blacks are more likely than other racial or ethnic groups to be characterized by whites as violent, more likely to abuse drugs, and more likely to engage in crime.[35] The results of another study corroborated the prevalence of this belief after finding that a majority of whites characterize Blacks as aggressive.[36] Other research has shown that the public perceives that Blacks are involved in a greater percentage of violent crime than official statistics indicate they actually are.[37]

In *Challenging Colorblind Education: A Descriptive Analysis of Teacher Racial Attitudes*, the authors found that African American students were treated less favorably by teachers and were less likely to be placed on the talented and gifted track than white students.[38] A national survey of more than 1,000 public school teachers found that the teaching population in 2011 was 84 percent white and 84 percent female. Many teachers have not had the experience or desire to respond effectively to African American students' cultural norms.[39] Many students in pre-service education programs enter the teaching profession with little previous contact with individuals from other racial backgrounds.[40] Black boys are seen as older and less innocent than their white, same age peers.[41]

Teachers perceived Black children in the primary grades as having more behavior problems and lower academic competencies than white students.[42] Instructors did not expect Black students in the secondary grades to perform as well as their white counterparts. School decision makers are more likely to interpret an African American student's conduct in an ambiguous situation as defiance, insubordination, or aggressive behavior that should be controlled by punitive school discipline.[43] This triggers the subtle conviction that behavior is threatening and dangerous when an African American individual engages in it compared to white students who engage in the same conduct.

The student-teacher relationship relies on trust and respect. Psychological research has indicated that youths are likely to disengage from school and academic pursuits when they perceive negative attitudes about themselves or their racial group in the school environment.[44] A stereotype that Black students are academically deficient and hostile to the teachers' goals can lead teachers to see Black students as "troublemakers" or menaces. With this mindset, teachers may respond more harshly to the conduct of Black students than toward identical behavior by white students.

Black students were referred more frequently to school psychologists, counselors, social workers, or hospitals for evaluation than white students. Teachers assumed that their Black students came from home environments in which parents did not value education. white teachers felt Black students were intimidating, and some admitted to being afraid of them. Other teachers confessed that they often tried not to speak to Black students or avoided eye contact with Black students. Some even admitted that they did not bother learning the names of African American students unless they were planning on writing a disciplinary note about their behavior. This sort of distancing and negativity creates an unwelcoming environment for Black students.

African American Females

Boys are not the only group suffering from negative images. In *Stereotype and School Pushout: Race, Gender, and Discipline Disparities*, Janel George explained that African American girls are subjected to race and gender stereotypes that influence school officials' responses to their behavior.[45] African American girls are penalized for deviating from gender norms and expectations of "feminine" behavior, which are based on models of white womanhood.[46]

Race and gender stereotypes about African American women are rooted in our nation's history and legacy of institutionalized racism. Stereotypes depicting African American women as seductive, hypersexual, and immoral were invoked to justify the sexual abuse and exploitation to which they were subjected. For African American girls, expectations in schools mirror the prevailing ideals of womanhood, which lead to social correction by teachers inculcated with these social norms and stereotypes.

Janel George explained that women and girls who are able to mirror normative expectations of femininity during their interactions with others are evaluated as appropriately feminine, "good" girls. Women and girls who are not perceived as fitting within normative expectations of femininity can suffer harsh consequences.[47] For African American girls who are perceived as not conforming to the ideals of womanhood in the school setting, the consequences can be punitive.[48]

African American girls are punished for their nonconformity to notions of white, middle-class femininity. Stereotypes of African American girls as assertive, loud, aggressive, and confrontational are used to justify the punitive sanctions. African American girls are often criticized for qualities that were developed to sustain their survival as Black females. Failing to conform to prevailing notions of femininity justifies punishment, and qualities of strength and resiliency developed by African American women to negotiate complicated social circumstances are devalued. Black girls must conform to white, middle-class notions of femininity by being quiet and passive, or speak up and get disciplined for defying those expectations and conforming to educators' stereotyped expectations for African American girls.

Unconscious stereotypes can create cultural barriers that separate Black students from white teachers.[49] Body language, accents, speech, dress, and behaviors of African American students are foreign and sometimes threatening to America's overwhelmingly white and female teaching force. Cultural misunderstandings between students and teachers can lead to unwarranted discipline for perceived unruliness. A lively debate may be interpreted as aggressive and contentious rather than the verbal sparring common among African American teenagers. Overlapping speech, such as the active "call-response" participatory pattern familiar to African American students, may be seen as disruptive and/or rude. Energetic horseplay may be mistakenly regarded as genuine aggression. Black females perceived as engaging in loud and defiant behavior may actually be manifesting important survival qualities that reflect resilience against racism, sexism, and classism.[50] For Black students, these disconnects are confusing when teachers sanction them for behavior that is accepted in their communities.

Another way in which implicit racial bias disadvantages minority students involves teachers' perceptions of student behavior.[51] Far too often, white teachers treat cultural differences as intellectual deficits and respond by imposing special education designations on a disproportionate number of Black students. Children in various cultures learn different rules for communicating with adults through facial expressions, body language, and physical gestures. In everyday conversation, spoken words are only one way to communicate. As little as seven percent of a message may be expressed in words. The rest is conveyed through facial expression, voice tone, body gestures, and overall posture. Unconscious bias can affect how behavior is perceived and interpreted. The research indicates that a teacher's race influences perceptions of students' behavior.[52] This unconscious process may be one of the reasons students of color often experience suspension in the absence of violent behavior.[53]

Much of the prevailing stereotypes about African American youth are the result of "cultural deficit thinking."[54] This causes many whites to believe that poor African American and other minority students and their parents are disconnected from the educational process. Teachers and administrators may harbor negative assumptions about the ability, aspirations, and work ethic of these students based on an assumption that they and their families do not value education in the same way it is valued by middle- and upper-class white students. This perception triggers a stereotype of low-income Black students as unruly, disruptive, and disrespectful.

The lawyers who argued Brown and their colleagues at the NAACP and other Civil Rights organizations assumed that they would encounter some difficulties in their efforts to implement Brown's mandate, but they also assumed that desegregation would ultimately proceed. However, the southern states reacted to Brown with a policy of "massive resistance." Senator Harry F. Byrd of Virginia promoted the *Declaration of Constitutional Principles*, which was known informally as the *Southern Manifesto*.[55] It was written in February and March 1956 and announced the southern states" opposition to racial integration of public places. Subsequently, school desegregation proceeded at a glacial pace. Ten years after *Brown*, only 1.2 percent of Black students in the South attended schools with whites.[56] In five states, Alabama, Mississippi, South Carolina, Florida, and Georgia, there were no Black students attending white schools.

Conclusion

By the late 1960s, the Brown's "deliberate speed" standard was finally abandoned.[57] Southern school districts were ordered to desegregate immediately and were obligated to prove they had removed all vestiges of segregation, "root and branch," before they could be released from federal court supervision of their desegregation efforts.[58] Federal courts approved a variety of plans to integrate schools, including busing to achieve racial balance in individual schools.[59] Desegregation remained an elusive goal as segregated housing patterns persisted. Neighborhood attendance zones would have resulted in segregated schools in most urban communities.[60]

Racial balance strategies proved to be a flawed measure of achieving racial equality.[61] The problem became the treatment of Black students inside integrated schools. De facto segregation was created in racially mixed schools as Black students tended to be relegated to the lower tracks while the talented and gifted programs became the reserve of affluent white students.[62] Black students are still being disciplined at astonishing rates.

Educational success entails a wide range of cultural behaviors including such non-academic attributes as comportment, dress, and accent.[63] Middle class children from suburban communities have learned this behavior, as have their teachers.[64] Children from low-income, inner-city backgrounds have not. Suburban students' speech, dress and mannerisms fit the expectations of their teachers. Urban students from low-income families are often seen as "difficult" and presenting "challenges."[65] However, both groups behave in accordance with the norms of the communities in which they reside.

What is seen as the "natural" ability of affluent students is, in reality, the product of the social and economic status of their parents. Privileged children are inculcated with speech patterns, styles of dress, and comportment that facilitate their success in the educational system. Their affluent backgrounds, conditioning, and experiences equip them with the attributes needed to reproduce their parents' social position. Too often, teachers erroneously interpret these class-based advantages as a reflection of "hard work" or "innate" ability. This is a reflection of implicit bias. Race and class intersect in ways that uniquely disadvantage Black students. The discipline disparities reflect a racial crisis in America's schools. Unconscious discrimination is the most significant factor in the persistent mistreatment of African American students.

Notes

1 347 US 483 (1954).

2 Civil Rights Data Collection, *US Dep't of Educ. Office for Civil rights, issue brief no. 1*, 1 Data Snapshot (School Discipline) 24 (2014). http://ocrdata.ed.gov/downloads/crdc-school-discipline-snapshot.pdf.

3 John T. Jost et al., *The Existence of Implicit Bias Is Beyond a Reasonable Doubt: A Refutation of Ideological and Methodological Objections and Executive Summary of Ten Studies That No Manager Should Ignore*, 29 Res. Organizational Behav. 39 (2009).

4 Samuel L. Gaertner and John F. Dovidio, *The Aversive Form of Racism, in* Prejudice, Discrimination and Racism: Theory and Research, 61–89 (John F. Dovidio and Samuel L. Gaertner, eds., 1986).

5 Jason P. Nance, *Over-Disciplining Students, Racial Bias, and the School-to-Prison Pipeline*, 50 Richmond L. R. 1067–70 (2016).

6 Ibid;; See also Lawrence Bobo and James Kluegel, *Status, Idealogy and Dimensions of White's Racial Beliefs and Attitudes: Progress and Stagnation, in* Racial Attitudes in the 1990s Continuity and Change, 99–105 (Steven A. Tuch and Jack K. Martin, eds., 1997).

7 Samuel L. Gaertner and John F. Dovidio, *Reducing Intergroup Bias: The Common Ingroup Identity Model*, 24–6 (2000).

8 Charles R. Lawrence, III, *The Id, the Ego, and Equal Protection: Reckoning with Unconscious Racism*, 39 Stan L. Rev. 317, 323 (1987).

9 Frances E. Aboud and Maria Amato, *Developmental and Socialization Influence on Intergroup Bias, in* Blackwell Handbook of Social Psychology: Intergroup Processes, 65–89 (Rupert Brown and Samuel Gaertner, eds., 2003).

10 Linda Hamilton Krieger, *The Content of Our Categories: A Cognitive Bias Approach to Discrimination and Equal Employment Opportunity*, 47 Stan. L. Rev. 1161 (1995); Jerry Kang, *Trojan Horses of Race*, 118 Harv. L. Rev. 1489–593 (2005).

11 See also Peggy C. Davis, *Law as Microaggression*, 98 Yale L. J. 1559, 1561–2 (1989) (explaining how racial stereotypes affect the cognitive processes of categorization in individuals).

12 Linda Hamilton Krieger and Susan T. Fiske, *Behavioral Realism in Employment Discrimination Law: Implicit Bias and Disparate Treatment*, 94 Calif. L. Rev. 997, 1034 (2006).

13 The tests were developed by Professors Anthony Greenwald and Mahzarin Banaji. See Project Implicit, IAT Home, at https://implicit.harvard.edu/implicit/demo/.

14 Christine Jolls and Cass R. Sunstein, *The Law of Implicit Bias*, 94 Calif. L. Rev. 969 (2006) (implicit bias should be controlled through a strategy of "debiasing" the law).

15 Audrey J. Lee, Note, *Unconscious Bias Theory in Employment Discrimination Litigation*, 40 Harv. C.R.-C.L. L. Rev. 481 (2005).

16 Anthony G. Greenwald, T. Andrew Poehlman, Eric Luis Uhlmann and Mahzarin R. Banaji, *Understanding and Using the Implicit Association Test: III. Meta-Analysis of Predictive Validity*, 97 JPPS. 17–41 (2009).

17 Thomas Dixon, *The Clansman: An Historical Romance of the Ku Klux* (Press of Braunworth & Co., 1970).

18 Charles Carroll, *"The Negro a Beast" or "In the Image of God"* (Lushena Books, 1900).

19 Elizabeth Ewen and Stuart Ewen, *Typecasting: On the Arts & Sciences of Human Inequality*, 407–13 (2006); J. Stanley Lemons, *Black Stereotypes as Reflected in Popular Culture, 1880–1920*, 29(1) Am. Quarterly 102–16 (1977).

20 At the turn of the century, Bert Williams and George Walker became the most popular Black performers in the United States. Marketing themselves as "Two Real Coons," Williams and Walker organized the first all-Black musical on Broadway, the 1903 production, *In Dahomey*. After Walker's death in 1909, Williams became the first Black artist featured in the Ziegfeld Follies. Louis Chude-Sokei. The Last "Darky": Bert Williams, *Black-On-Black Minstrelsy, and the African Diaspora* (2005).

21 Donald Bogle, *Toms, Coons, Mulattoes, Mammies, and Bucks: An Interpretive History of Blacks in American Films* (Bloomsbury Academic, 1989).

22 *The Little Colonel* (1935); *The Littlest Rebel* (1935); *Rebecca of Sunnybrook Farm* (1938).

23 Lincoln Theodore Perry's character, Stepin Fetchit, is a classic portrayal of the Coon. See *In Old Kentucky* (1929); *Stand Up and Cheer* (1934), *David Harum* (1934).

24 *Gone With the Wind* (1939).

25 *Imitation of Life* (1934 and 1959); *Pinky* (1949).

26 *Birth of a Nation* (1915).

27 The Wilson administration implemented segregation in federal government. Wilson allowed officials to segregate the toilets, cafeterias, and work areas in their departments. Most Black diplomats were replaced by whites, Black federal officials in the South were removed from their posts, and the District of Columbia police force and fire departments stopped hiring Blacks. Nicholas Patler, *Jim Crow and the Wilson Administration: Protesting Federal Segregation in the Early Twentieth Century* (University Press of Colorado, 2004).

28 *Song of the South* (1946).

29 See generally Joel Chandler Harris, *Uncle Remus; Tales* (Beehive Press, 1974).

30 Donald Bogle, *Primetime Blues: African Americans on Network Television*, 26–42 (Farrar, Straus, and Giroux, 2001).

Marilyn Kern-Foxworth, *Aunt Jemima, Uncle Ben, and Rastus: Blacks in Advertising, Yesterday, Today, and Tomorrow* (Praeger Publishers, 1994) (describing the historical evolution of African Americans in advertising and explains how the images of Aunt Jemima, Uncle Ben, and Rastus promoted negative stereotyping).

32 Examples of cartoon images can be viewed at the Jim Crow Museum, Ferris State University, www.ferris.edu/htmls/news/jimcrow/menu.htm.

33 Randolph G. Potts, *The Social Construction and Social Marketing of the "Dangerous Black Man,"* 2 J. Afr. Am. Men 4 (1997); Helán E. Page, *"Black Male" Imagery and Media Containment of African American Men*, 99(1) Am. Anthropologist 99–111 (1997).

34 Dennis Rome, *Black Demons: The Media's Depiction of the African American Male Criminal Stereotype* (2004); Lawrence D. Bobo, *Racial Attitudes and Relations at the Close of the Twentieth Century*, in America Becoming: Racial Trends and Their Consequences, 264, 273–80 (Neil J. Smelser, William Julius Wilson, and Faith Mitchell, eds., 2001); David J. Knight, *Beyond the Stereotypical Image of Young Men of Color*, The Atlantic (Jan 5, 2015), http://www.theatlantic.com/education/archive/2015/01/beyond-the-stereotypical-image-of-young-men-of-color/384194/.

35 Lee Sigelman and Steven A. Tuch, *Metastereotypes: Blacks' Perceptions of Whites' Stereotypes of Blacks*, 61 Public Opinion Quarterly 87–101 (1996).

36 Jon Hurwitz and Mark Peffley (eds.), *Perception and Prejudice: Race and Politics in the United States* (Yale University Press, 1998).

37 Kelly Welch, *Black Criminal Stereotypes and Racial Profiling*, 23 J. Contemp. Crim. Jus. 276, 278 (2007).

38 Melanie S. Hinojosa and Amanda Mora, *Challenging Colorblind Education: A Descriptive Analysis of Teacher Racial Attitudes,* 4(2) Sociol Faculty Publications 28–30 (2009), http://digitalcommons.sacredheart.edu/cgi/viewcontent.cgi?article=1005&context=sociol_fac.

39 Ibid.

40 Prudence Carter, Russell Skiba, Mariella Arredondo and Mica Pollock, *You Can't Fix What You Don't Look At: Acknowledging Race in Addressing Racial Discipline Disparities* (2014), http://www.indiana.edu/~atlantic/wp-content/uploads/2014/12/Acknowledging-Race_121514.pdf.

41 Phillip Atiba et al., *The Essence of Innocence: Consequences of Dehumanizing Black*, 106 Children J. of Pers. and Soc. Psych., 526, 531 (2014).

42 *Perception and Prejudice: Race and Politics in the United States, supra* note 129.

43 David Simson, *Exclusion, Punishment, Racism and Our Schools: A Critical Race Theory Perspective on School Discipline*, 61 UCLA L. Rev. 506, 547 (2014).

44 Michael Roque and Raymond Paternoster, *Understanding the Antecedents of the "School to Jail" Link: The Relationship Between Race and School Discipline*, 101 J. Crim. L. & Criminol. 633, 636–7 (2011).

45 Janel A. George, *Stereotype and School Pushout: Race, Gender, and Discipline Disparities*, 68 Ark. L. Rev. 101, 107–9 (2015).

46 Ibid; See also Edward W. Morris, *"Ladies" or "Loudies"? Perceptions and Experiences of Black Girls in Classrooms*, 38 Youth & SOC'Y 490 (2007).

47 Ibid; See also Edward W. Morris, *"Tuck in that Shirt!" Race, Class, Gender, and Discipline in an Urban School*, 48 Sociol. Perspectives 25–48 (2005).

48 Jamilia J. Blake et al., *Unmasking the Inequitable Discipline Experiences of Urban Black Girls: Implications for Urban Educational Stakeholders*, 43(1) Urban Rev. 90–106 (2010).

49 Roque and Paternoster, *Understanding the Antecedents of the "School to Jail" Link*, *supra* note 55.

50 The "code of the street" is an informal system that regulates social interactions in low income neighborhoods. In economically deprived communities, the code of the street is a component of a subculture that governs behavior, particularly violence. Poor, inner-city residents are forced to abide by the code of the street as a survival mechanism. Functioning in this subculture requires an aggressive demeanor. Individuals must gain respect from others by projecting a "hard" image which is an essential to how people are perceived and respected in the community. See Elijah Anderson, The Code of the Streets, *The Atlantic Monthly*, May 1994, http://www.theatlantic.com/magazine/archive/1994/05/the-code-of-the-streets/306601/.

51 Cheryl Staats, *Kirwan Institute for the Study of Race and Ethnicity, Implicit Racial Bias and School Discipline Disparities: Exploring the Connection 8,9* (Kirwan Institute Special Report, 2014), https://kirwaninstitute.osu.edu/sites/default/files/documents/ki-ib-argument-piece03.pdf).

52 Seth Gershenson, Stephen B. Holt and Nicholas W. Papageorge, *Who Believes in Me? The Effect of Student–Teacher Demographic Match on Teacher Expectations*, Upjohn Institute Working Paper 15-231. (Kalamazoo, MI: W.E. Upjohn Institute for Employment Research, 2015). https://doi.org/10.17848/wp15-231.

53 Cheryl Staats, *Kirwan Institute for the Study of Race*, *supra* note 160.

54 Kirwan Institute for the Study of Race and Ethnicity, *Racial Disproportionality in School Discipline: Implicit Bias is Heavily Implicated* (2014), http://kirwaninstitute.osu.edu/racial-disproportionality-in-school-discipline-implicit-bias-is-heavily-implicated.

55 See 102 Cong. Rec. 4459–61 (1956), http://history.house.gov/Historical-Highlights/1951-2000/The-Southern-Manifesto-of-1956/.

56 Leland Ware, *Deliberate Speed: Implementing Brown's Ambiguous Mandate,* 22 Delaware Lawyer 26 (2004).

57 *Griffin v. School Board*, 377 US 218 (1964).

58 *Green v. County Sch. Bd. of New Kent County*, 391 US 430 (1968).

59 *Swann v. Charlotte-Mecklenburg Board of Education*, 402 US 1 (1971).

60 See, e.g., *Parents Involved* in *Community Schools v. Seattle School District No. 1*, 551 US 701 (2007). Douglas S. Massey and Nancy A. Denton, *American Apartheid: Segregation and the Making of the Underclass* (Harvard University Press, 1993); John Iceland et al., *US Census Bureau, CENSR-3, Racial and Ethnic Residential Segregation in the United States: 1980–2000* (2002), https://www.census.gov/prod/2002pubs/censr-3.pdf.

61 Melva Ware, *The Racial Balance Standard Is an Inadequate Approach to Achieving Racial Equality in Schools* 18 St. Louis U. Pub. L. Rev. 465 (1999).

62 Allison Roda, *Inequality in Gifted and Talented Programs, Parental Choices about Status, School Opportunity, and Second-Generation Segregation* (Palgrave Macmillan, 2015); In Houston's Gifted Program, Critics Say Blacks and Latinos Are Overlooked, *NPR*, Sept. 30, 2015, http://www.npr.org/sections/ed/2015/09/30/441409122/in-houstons-gifted-program-blacks-and-latinos-are-underrepresented.

63 See generally La Vonne Neal et al., *The Effects of African American Movement Styles on Teachers' Perceptions and Reactions*, 37, J. Special Educ. 49 (2003); Edward W. Morris, *supra* note 147.

64 See also Cynthia S. Glass, *Perception of Misbehavior: Understanding the Process of Labeling and the Role of Cultural Capital in the Disciplinary Process,* Urban Review, 46, 373–6 (2014).

65 See generally Ann Arnett Ferguson, *Bad Boys: Public Schools and the Making of Black Masculinity* (The University of Michigan Press, 2000).

5

The Great Migration and Suburban Segregation

After *Milliken v. Bradley*,[1] Suburban School districts were effectively protected from school desegregation efforts. School desegregation proceeded within school districts, relying heavily on busing to achieve racial balance. After the end of the South's "massive resistance" to desegregation in the late 1960s, residential segregation thwarted efforts to desegregate public schools. The federal government played an essential role in the development, institutionalization, and perpetuation of neighborhood segregation.

When northern and Midwestern cities began to industrialize at the beginning of the twentieth century, thousands of African American families migrated from the rural south.[2] They were "pushed" by the violence and intimidation in the segregated South and "pulled" by the lure of better-paying factory jobs and a higher standard of living. Like the foreign immigrants who were pouring in from Europe, Blacks worked in factories in a rapidly industrializing economy.

When Black migrants arrived in urban communities, they encountered many obstacles. Municipal ordinances were enacted that prohibited African Americans from occupying properties except in designated neighborhoods. In 1910, Baltimore became the first city in America to adopt a residential segregation ordinance.[3] The laws were challenged and declared unconstitutional as violations of the Fourteenth Amendment in a 1917 decision, *Buchanan v. Warley*.[4]

After *Buchanan*, the real estate industry devised another tactic: racially restrictive covenants. The covenants were clauses in deeds that prohibited property owners and subsequent purchasers from selling their homes to racial and religious minorities. The Supreme Court implicitly endorsed the covenants in a 1926 decision, *Corrigan v. Buckley*.[5] The Fourteenth Amendment applies only to "state action" which consists of actions taken by state and local governments. The Court did not decide the merits of *Corrigan*, but it issued an opinion that stated the Fourteenth Amendment did not prohibit private parties from controlling the use and disposition of their property.

As the northern migration continued, an already severe housing shortage for African Americans worsened. Blacks were crowded into existing ghettos that expanded as whites moved out of adjacent neighborhoods. Overcrowding created financial incentives to violate the covenants. In many cases, a white "strawman" purchased a property and immediately resold it to a Black purchaser, usually at a significant profit. In the 1940s, the National Association for the Advancement of Colored People (NAACP) launched a formal litigation campaign that challenged restrictive covenants. In 1948, the Supreme Court held in *Shelley v. Kraemer*[6] that restrictive covenants were private arrangements, but the judicial enforcement of discriminatory agreements constituted state action that violated the Fourteenth Amendment. After *Shelley*, the covenants could not be enforced in courts. This was an important but largely symbolic victory for the NAACP.[7] Discriminatory practices continued.

The American middle class emerged during the post-Second World War era.[8] Before the war, working-class whites lived in ethnic enclaves in cities or in small towns and rural communities. Extended families often occupied the same residence. The 1944 G.I. Bill provided returning veterans with financial assistance for college and home mortgages. Millions of servicemen were able to afford homes for the first time. In 1947, real estate developer William Levitt purchased 4,000 acres of farmland on Long Island, New York, and converted it into the largest privately planned community in American history.

Suburban communities could not have been constructed without the federal government's support. Communities like Levittown were constructed in metropolitan regions across the nation. Residential construction rose from 114,000 new homes in 1944 to 1.7 million by 1950.[9] All of this was facilitated by the introduction of fixed-rate, thirty-year mortgages insured by the Veterans Administration and the Federal Housing Authority.[10] Mortgage interest and local property taxes could be deducted from federal income taxes. In many cases, buying a home was cheaper than renting. Middle-class American families could achieve the American dream, a single family, detached home on a quarter-acre lot.

During the postwar era, a distinct image of American family life was promoted. The family unit consisted of a husband, wife, and two or three children. Prior to the war, intergenerational families lived in a single household. Many of them lived in ethnic enclaves that were settled during the first decades of the twentieth century.[11] They maintained many of the customs, languages, and religious traditions of the countries from which they migrated. The suburbs facilitated conformity and assimilation. A 1954 *Saturday Evening Post* article described Levittown: "Everybody lives on the same side of the tracks. They have no slums to fret about, no families of conspicuous wealth to envy, no traditional upper crust to whet and thwart their social aspirations."[12]

In newspapers, magazine advertisements, and television programs, images of the ideal American family were presented. The image presented on American television shows was the picture-perfect family consisting of the breadwinning, middle-class father, a doting housewife who was content to clean the house and cook the family's meals. Their children never seemed to get into trouble that could not be fixed. A generation of children learned to read in books that depicted Dick and Jane and their dog Spot. The characters resided in a suburban home surrounded by a white picket fence.[13] Popular television shows like *The Adventures of Ozzie & Harriet*, *Leave It to Beaver*, and *Father Knows Best* depicted images of wholesome, all-American families. Norman Rockwell's paintings adorned the covers of popular magazines. They were idealized and sentimental visions of American life.[14] African Americans were conspicuously absent from these images.

Housing segregation was mandated by the federal government. The Home Owners' Loan Corporation (HOLC), a federal agency established during the 1930s depression, fostered residential segregation through "redlining."[15] Land economists believed that property values were closely linked to the racial composition of neighborhoods. The HOLC rated every neighborhood in America "A," "B," "C," or "D" using color coded maps. The lowest quality rating, "D," was colored red. Neighborhoods rated "A" had to be homogeneous and occupied by the families of business and professional men who were white and usually native-born. Neighborhoods in which Blacks resided were rated "D" and coded red. Lenders were discouraged from making loans in neighborhoods that were redlined.[16] The HOLC neighborhood risk maps institutionalized discrimination based on race and geography.

The FHA used HOLC's system to develop criteria for selecting the mortgages it would insure. The FHA's underwriting standards reflected the model of neighborhood change developed by economist Homer Hoyt. In his influential 1939 book *The Structure and Growth of Residential Neighborhoods in American Cities*, Hoyt described the patterns of development of residential neighborhoods according to his "sector theory" of neighborhood change.[17]

According to Hoyt's sector theory, areas developed along certain sections of a city. A high-grade residential area was the center of attraction that pulled other residential areas toward it. However, if a high-rent district was established in another sector, other high-rent districts would extend out from that point and pull the growth of the city in that direction while lower-income groups moved into the houses in older neighborhoods. In this invasion-succession model, newly constructed neighborhoods were occupied by white families. [18] Over time, the neighborhood transitioned from white Protestant to Jewish families and finally to African Americans as the housing stock grew older and began to deteriorate. Hoyt wrote:

> [i]f the entrance of a colored family into a white neighborhood causes a general exodus of the white people it is reflected in property values. Except in the case of Negroes and Mexicans, however, these racial and national barriers disappear when the individuals of the foreign nationality groups rise in the economic scale or conform to the American standards of living. . . . While the ranking may be scientifically wrong from the standpoint of inherent racial characteristics, it registers an opinion or prejudice that is reflected in land values; it is the ranking of race and nationalities with respect to their beneficial effect upon land values. Those having the most favorable effect come first in the list and those exerting the most detrimental effect appear last: 1. English, Germans, Scots, Irish, Scandinavians 2. North Italians 3. Bohemians or Czechoslovakians 3. Poles 4. Lithuanians 5. Greeks 6. Russian Jews of lower class 6. South Italians 6. Negroes 7. Mexicans.[19]

The FHA developed Residential Security Maps that assigned every neighborhood a place somewhere along this continuum.[20] The FHA's

Underwriting Manual warned lenders that neighborhoods could retain their values only if the properties were occupied by the same social classes and racial groups. The agency urged the use of restrictive covenants to maintain neighborhood stability. The FHA's 1935 *Underwriting Manual* stated, "If a neighborhood is to retain stability it is necessary that properties shall continue to be occupied by the same social and racial classes. A change in social or racial occupancy generally leads to instability and a reduction in value." The 1939 FHA Underwriting Manual on Racial Restrictive Covenants stated:

> The Valuator should realize that the need for protection from adverse influences is greater in an undeveloped or partially developed area than in any other type of neighborhood. Generally, a high rating should be given only where adequate and enforced zoning regulations exist or where effective restrictive covenants are recorded against the entire tract, since these provide the surest protection against undesirable encroachment and inharmonious use. To be most effective, deed restrictions should be imposed upon all land in the immediate environment of the subject location. . . . Recommended restrictions should include provisions for the following... Prohibition of the occupancy of properties except by the race for which they are intended.[21]

After the decision in *Shelley v. Kraemer*, the FHA made some largely cosmetic changes to its *Underwriting Manual*. Explicit references to race were removed. However, the *Manual* continued to warn against the introduction of adverse influences that would diminish the desirability of the neighborhood or lower property values. Local real estate boards warned members not to introduce elements into a neighborhood that would be detrimental to property values and explicitly included Blacks among the undesirable elements. Real estate publications used in college and university courses and by practicing realtors continued to urge separating "inharmonious" populations.

Revised editions of *Hoyt's Principles of Urban Real Estate*[22] toned down some of its racial references but did not abandon its message that white neighborhoods needed protection from "inharmonious groups." Home equity is the principal source of wealth for most American families. The federal government's discriminatory policies excluded African Americans from the largest wealth-producing programs in the nation's history; single-family homes in suburban communities purchased with VA and FHA insured mortgages.[23] The Black/white wealth disparities are largely the product of post-Second World War government policies that excluded African Americans.

When *Brown* was decided, neighborhoods were already segregated after decades of discriminatory practices that the federal government mandated. In the 1940s and 1950s, white families that resided in cities were rapidly moving to the surrounding suburbs. With the advent of school desegregation, "white flight" to suburban communities accelerated. A demographic pattern developed that continues into the present. Black families were confined to large, continuous settlements of densely inhabited neighborhoods that are tightly packed around the urban core. Whites lived in suburban neighborhoods with separate school districts. This frustrated school desegregation efforts in urban communities.

Urban Renewal

The Housing Act of 1949 had the ambitious goal "[to] provide a decent home and suitable environment for every American family."[24] Despite its lofty aspirations, the Act facilitated the use of urban renewal programs to create and sustain racially separate neighborhoods. Efforts to develop federal housing policies began in the mid-1920s when the market for the development of land in cities was shrinking as a result of the movement of middle-income families and industry to surrounding areas. Neighborhoods adjacent to the CBD contained deteriorating buildings, decreased occupancy, and unsafe structures. Downtown business owners feared that property values in the CBD would decline rapidly. These areas were low-income neighborhoods occupied by recent immigrants and racial minorities. Redlining and restrictive covenants confined African American families to geographically compact areas near the CBD that had the oldest buildings and infrastructure.

Downtown business owners and civic groups wanted large areas to be redeveloped for high-end commercial and residential uses surrounded by parks, efficient transportation systems, and attractive amenities. Proposals were made that included enacting state laws empowering municipalities to redevelop declining and dilapidated areas adjacent to central business districts. They argued that the transition could be accomplished by the demolition of the existing structures, followed by large-scale rebuilding. Sizable tracts of land had to be assembled within a reasonable time at an affordable price. The redevelopment proposals included public-private coordination of urban land use, long-term federal loans to cities at low interest rates, and generous tax subsidies and write-offs for local redevelopers. This approach became the core of urban revitalization programs throughout the nation.

The acquisition of large contiguous tracts was difficult because of the various parties and interests that owned and controlled the properties. The solution was the use of local governments' eminent domain powers to acquire the land and resell it to private corporations at a discounted price coupled with tax abatements. Local governments were expected to bear the cost of amenities such as new street systems, transportation facilities, schools, playgrounds, buildings, and utilities such as water and sewer lines.

The Housing Act of 1937 authorized local communities to create housing authorities with the legal power of eminent domain to acquire privately owned land for slum clearance and new construction. After the Housing Act of 1954 was adopted, cities could use federal funds to build new housing in cleared areas and to pay private developers to construct highways, office buildings, and shopping malls.

Local real estate officials and downtown business elites viewed the Housing Act as a mechanism for eliminating blighted areas surrounding the central business district and using federal subsidies to engineer downtown redevelopment and growth. The Act stipulated that major urban cities would receive funds to renovate blighted areas, including neighborhoods classified as slums and buildings deemed unsafe and uninhabitable. In *Berman v. Parker*[25] the District of Columbia's Planning Commission proposed to begin redevelopment in the southwestern area of the city. In that section, approximately 5,000 persons resided, 98 percent of whom were African American. Surveys prepared for the commission found that only 58 percent of the dwellings had outdoor toilets. More than 80 percent had no central heating, and 29 percent had no electricity.

Included in the property to be condemned was a department store in reasonably good condition. The store's owners sued arguing that the store posed no threat to public order, health, or safety. The Supreme Court held that when a locality determines that the post-redevelopment use of private property has a public purpose, it is free to employ reasonable means to ensure that the purpose is promoted.

Urban renewal projects were intended to condemn slum neighborhoods, tear down the buildings, and resell the cleared land to private developers at a reduced price. In addition to relocating the residents to safe and sanitary housing, the program was intended to stimulate large-scale private rebuilding, add new tax revenues for cities, revitalize their downtown areas, and halt white flight to the suburbs. Local housing authorities constructed low-income housing developments in segregated, inner-city neighborhoods. Because urban renewal was intended to clear areas of concentrated poverty, low-income families and minorities were disproportionately impacted.[26] Public housing was expected to replace the homes that were razed, but the new projects did not have enough units to house the displaced families.[27]

During the late 1950s and 1960s, high-rise projects dominated the design of American public housing. Housing officials in America and Europe were inspired by Le Corbusier's visions of towers rising out of vast expanses of grass and greenery. Le Corbusier, a Swiss-born modernist-architect, exerted a powerful influence on a generation of designers who were mesmerized by his bold drawings of what he called the *Cité radieuse* (radiant city.)[28] The movement for modernism also gained support from city officials and developers who saw sleek skyscrapers as a way of modernizing the aging urban landscapes of post-war America. Public housing consisted largely of the Brutalist style, which evolved from the modernist architectural movement of the early twentieth century.[29]

Public housing contributed to social problems because it concentrated impoverished families in high-density, multi-family dwellings. The housing projects erected to replace slums soon became dilapidated and crime ridden. They were disproportionately home to poor, single-parent households. Many projects became lawless places, overrun with gang activities. They were a cold and alienating urban presence. Among some tenants, a feeling of bei crowded into housing with other tenants from similar backgrounds made some residents feel that they were being excluded from mainstream society. In many cases, insufficient funding and poor management caused many developments to fall into disrepair. Urban renewal was labeled "Negro removal" because of the ways it destroyed many thriving, Black communities.[30] An estimated eighty percent of the people displaced were African Americans.[31]

Low-income, multifamily housing developments intensified racial and economic segregation. The Housing Act of 1949 intended to relieve a housing shortage, but the program destroyed thousands more units than it replaced and dislocated tens of thousands of small businesses and residents. In 1974, the federal government discontinued the urban renewal program amid widespread urban protest and neighborhood discontent about the destabilizing effects of the program on inner-city communities.[32]

The Interstate Highway System

In 1919, Lieutenant Colonel Dwight Eisenhower participated in a transcontinental convoy organized by the US Army Motor Transport Corps. The group traveled 3,000 miles from Washington, D.C., to Oakland, California, and by ferry to San Francisco. The participants encountered difficult conditions. Half the distance was over dirt roads, wheel paths, desert sands, and mountain trails. There were many accidents. Trucks sank in quicksand or mud, ran off the road, or overturned. The convoy encountered inadequate bridges, a lack of food, shelter, and bathing facilities, and inadequate drinking water. That experience inspired Eisenhower's belief that a national highway system was needed. During the Second World War, General Eisenhower was stationed in Germany, where he was impressed by the network of high-speed roads known as the Reichsautobahnen. After he was elected president in 1952, Eisenhower was determined to build a system of interstate highways.

The interstate highway system revolutionized transportation, but it inflicted irreparable damage on urban neighborhoods.[33] The roads displaced families from their homes, sliced communities in half, and led to abandonment and decay in urban communities.[34] On June 26, 1956, Congress passed the

Federal-Aid Highway Act of 1956. Revenue from federal gas and other motor vehicle taxes was credited to the Highway Trust Fund to pay the federal share of interstate construction and all other federally aided highway projects. The intent was that the program would be self-financing.

Interstate highways are controlled-access expressways with no at-grade crossings. They have overpasses and underpasses instead of intersections. They are at least four lanes wide and designed for high-speed driving. They were intended to eliminate traffic congestion, replace undesirable slum areas with attractive roadways, and make transportation more efficient. The interstates made travel in and out of American cities simpler and sped the growth of suburbs. The highways increased the mobility of Americans, allowing them to move out of cities and establish homes in suburban communities and to travel quickly from one region to another for vacation and business.

The Highway Act authorized the construction of a 41,000-mile network of interstate highways and allocated $26 billion to pay for them. The 1956 Act set the federal share for interstate construction at 90 percent in recognition of the national scope of the project. Each state transportation department managed its own program for location, design, right-of-way acquisition, and construction. The states are responsible for the ownership and maintenance of the system.

Local officials used highways to separate Black and white neighborhoods, reinforcing residential segregation.[35] Interstate highway construction destroyed entire neighborhoods and isolated others, creating inner-city ghettos. As former US Department Transportation Secretary Anthony Foxx explained:

> The interstate highway system is at once a marvel of ingenuity and efficiency . . . and an example of how physical barriers can create and exacerbate social ones. No city was spared the system's effects, largely affecting minority and low-income areas in Detroit, New Orleans, Los Angeles, Chicago, New York City, and my hometown, Charlotte [North Carolina]. . . . Many routes cut through the hearts of low-income and minority communities, often in conjunction with urban renewal programs that purported to remove urban blight. There are numerous examples of ensuing disparate impacts, be it the Dan Ryan Expressway in Chicago separating the Robert Taylor homes (an iconic, largely African American housing project constructed in the late

1950s and demolished in the mid-2000s) from the rest of the city or I-95 displacing 1,093 (out of 1,289) minority families in Camden, New Jersey.[36]

The combination of cars, highways, concrete, and oil made central cities the chief casualty of suburbanization. The combination of urban renewal's demolition and the construction of interstate highways turned many central city communities into ominous, dystopian landscapes of poverty and despair.

Exclusionary Zoning

Local governments have the legal authority to regulate the use of land within their borders. Over the years, they have used their zoning powers to perpetuate segregated neighborhoods. New York City was the first municipality to enact zoning ordinances.[37] In *Euclid v. Ambler Realty*,[38] the Supreme Court held that municipalities could regulate private property even if the zoning decreases the value of the property. This case gave rise to the concept of "Euclidean Zoning," a system in which a municipality is divided into areas where specific uses of land are permitted. Planners believed that the uses to which land was dedicated should be separated. This meant, for example, that one area within a municipality would be devoted to factories, another to retail and commercial developments. Other areas would be devoted to farmland, and finally specific areas would be limited to residential uses.

In residential areas, disputes arose concerning the zoning that tended to exclude African Americans. A typical example of exclusionary zoning is a limitation of residential development to single-family housing on large lots. This practice has been challenged because it excludes a disproportionate proportion of racial minorities. In *Village of Arlington Heights v. Metropolitan Housing Development Corp*,[39] a development organization applied to the Village of Arlington Heights for rezoning of a fifteen-acre parcel from single-family residential to multi-family residential, intending to build federally subsidized low-income housing.

After the request was denied, a civil action was filed claiming that the denial of rezoning violated the Fourteenth Amendment and the Fair Housing Act.

The Supreme Court held that a municipality's zoning decision would not be held unconstitutional solely because it had a racially disproportionate impact. The development organization did not prove that the zoning board acted with a discriminatory intent, which is required to prevail on a claim alleging a violation of the Equal Protection Clause of the Fourteenth Amendment.[40]

In *Huntington Branch, NAACP v. Town of Huntington*[41] a suit was filed by a developer claiming that the New Jersey township violated the Fair Housing Act by restricting private construction of multi-family housing to a narrow urban renewal area and refusing to rezone the parcel outside of this area where the organization desired to build multi-family housing. The district court refused to invalidate the zoning restriction. The appellate court held that the zoning restriction had a discriminatory effect and that the town had not shown a legitimate justification for its actions that outweighed the adverse effect.

In *Southern Burlington County N.A.A.C.P. v. Township of Mount Laurel*[42] a civil action was filed challenging the township's system of land use regulation on the grounds that low and moderate-income families were unlawfully excluded from the municipality. The New Jersey Supreme Court held that a municipality may not, by a system of land use regulation, make it physically and economically impossible to provide low and moderate-income housing in the township. The ordinance permitting only single-family detached dwellings was so restrictive in its minimum lot area, lot frontage, and building size requirements that it precluded single-family housing for even moderate-income families, which was contrary to the state's general welfare.[43]

The Court ordered all New Jersey municipalities to take affirmative actions to provide realistic opportunities for their fair share of the region's need for affordable housing for low- and moderate-income people. The state subsequently enacted legislation requiring municipalities to enact zoning that facilitates the construction of affordable housing.

Conclusion

Segregation is a tool that was used to promote and preserve white supremacy. Racial separation makes it easier to isolate, surveil, and police Black people concentrated in inner-city communities. *Plessy v. Ferguson* provided the legal foundation for discriminatory structures that continue to burden the lived experiences of African Americans.

Substantial progress has been made since the enactment of the Civil Rights laws of the 1960s. There has been significant progress in eliminating vestiges of segregation, but the pace of progress has been slow. As one study explains:

> Residential segregation has generally slowly declined over the past several decades following the passage of the 1968 Fair Housing Act. Yet today it remains a pressing issue throughout many areas of the country. . . . Of the different demographic groups examined, by far the highest levels of segregation were between non-Hispanic whites and blacks. The Milwaukee-Waukesha, Wisc., metro area recorded the highest dissimilarity index, followed by New York, Chicago and Detroit-Warren-Dearborn, Mich. Nationally, the median black-white dissimilarity index—which ranges from 0 (fully integrated) to 1 (fully segregated)—was 0.526. [44]

The Black population residing in US cities has steadily declined for decades. Between 1970 and 1995, 7 million Blacks moved to suburban communities. This number is considerably larger than the 4.5 million Blacks who moved from the South to the North during the Great Migration in the first half of the twentieth century. The percentage of African Americans living in urban cores shrank from 47 to 41.7 percent between 1990 and 2017. The Black population of the central cities in the nation's 100 largest metropolitan areas declined by 300,000 between 2000 and 2010. By 2010, most African Americans nationwide lived in suburban communities.

Affluent Black families have moved to suburban communities, leaving lower income families in impoverished, inner-city neighborhoods. The architecture of America's built environment reflects decades of government-sponsored segregation. High levels of residential separation persist, causing public schools in urban communities to remain segregated. African Americans and Latino/as possess less wealth than whites, fewer opportunities for upward mobility, lower income levels, and fewer chances to build wealth. This is *Plessy's* legacy.

Notes

1 *Milliken v. Bradley*, 418 US 717 (1974).

2 Isabel Wilkerson, *The Warmth of Other Suns: The Epic Story of America's Great Migration* (Random House, 2010); Nicholas Lemann, *The Promised Land: The Great Migration and How It Changed America* (Vintage Books, 1991); Gunnar Myrdal, *An American Dilemma: The Negro Problem and Modern Democracy* (Transaction Publishers, 1944).

3 Garrett Power, *Apartheid Baltimore Style: The Residential Segregation Ordinances of 1910–1913*, 42 Md. L. Rev. 289 (1983), http://digitalcommons.law.umaryland .edu/mlr/vol42/iss2/4.

4 *Buchanan v. Warley*, 245 US 60 (1917). (Basing ruling on the rights of whites to sell their property to whomever they wished rather than the equality rights of African Americans).

5 *Corrigan v. Buckley*, 271 US 323 (1926).

6 *Shelley v. Kraemer*, 334 US 1 (1948).

7 Leland Ware, *Invisible Walls: An Examination of the Legal Strategy of the Restrictive Covenant Cases*, 67 Wash. U. L.Q. 737, 738 (1989); Leland Ware and Theodore Davis, *Ordinary People in an Extraordinary Time: The Black Middle-Class in the Age of Obama*, 55 How. L. J. 533 (2012).

8 Douglas S. Massey and Nancy A. Denton, American Apartheid: Segregation and the Making of the Underclass, *Harvard University Press*, 1993; Reprint edition; Richard Rothstein, *The Color of Law: A Forgotten History of How Our Government Segregated America* (Liveright, 2017); Kenneth Fox, *Metropolitan America: Urban Life and Urban Policy in the United States, 1940–1980* (1990).

9 Claire A. Suddath, Brief History of the Middle Class, *Time Magazine*, Feb. 27, 2009, http://content.time.com/time/nation/article/0,8599,1882147,00.html.

10 Massey and Denton, American Apartheid, *supra* note 8; Leland Ware, *A Century of Segregation: Race, Class, and Disadvantage* (2018); Kenneth T. Jackson, *Crabgrass Frontier: The Suburbanization of the United States* (1985); David M. P. Freund, *Colored Property: State Policy and white Racial Politics in Suburban America* (2010).

11 Herbert J. Gans, *Symbolic Ethnicity: The Future of Ethnic Groups and Cultures in America*, 2(1) Ethnic Racial Stud.1–20 (1979), doi:10.1080/01419870.1979.9993248.

12 http://statemuseumpa.org/levittown/two/i.html.

13 Adalaide Morris, *Dick, Jane, and American Literature: Fighting with Canons*, 47(5) College English 467–81 (1985). doi:10.2307/376878.
14 What's My Rockwell Worth? FAQ, *NRM.org*, https://www.nrm.org/about/whats-rockwell-worth-faq/.
15 Melvin L. Oliver and Thomas M. Shapiro, *Black Wealth/White Wealth: A New Perspective on Racial Inequality* (Taylor & Francis, 1997); Richard Rothstein, *The Color of Law: A Forgotten History of How Our Government Segregated America* (Liveright, 2017).
16 Benjamin Howell, *Exploiting Race and Space: Concentrated Subprime Lending as Housing Discrimination*, 94 Calif. L. Rev. 101, 112 (2006).
17 Homer Hoyt, *The Structure and Growth of Residential Neighborhoods in American Cities* (Federal Housing Administration, 1939).
18 Adam Gordon, *The Creation of Homeownership: How New Deal Changes in Banking Regulation Simultaneously Made Homeownership Accessible to Whites and Out of Reach for Blacks*, 186 Yale L.J. 115, 207 (2005).
19 Homer Hoyt, *One Hundred Years of Land Values in Chicago* (public domain, 1933).
20 Robert K. Nelson, LeDale Winling, Richard Marciano, Nathan Connolly, et al., Mapping Inequality: Redlining in New Deal America, *American Panorama*, https://dsl.richmond.edu/panorama/redlining/#loc=4/36.71/-96.93&opacity=0.8.
21 Robert Weaver, The Negro Ghetto, *New York: Harcourt, Brace and Company*, 1948, 72. Originally in Federal Housing Administration, 1939. "Underwriting Manual." Sections 932 and 935.
22 Arthur M. Weimer and Homer Hoyt, *Principles of Urban Real Estate* (Ronald Press Company, 1939; 2nd ed., 1948; 3rd ed., 1954).
23 Melvin Oliver and Thomas Shapiro, *Black Wealth/White Wealth: A New Perspective on Racial Inequality* (New York: Routledge, 1995).
24 Congressional declaration of national housing policy. 42 US Code § 1441.
25 *Berman v. Parker*, 348 US 26 (1954).
26 Martin Anderson, *The Federal Bulldozer: A Critical Analysis of Urban Renewal, 1949–1962* (Cambridge, MA: M.I.T. Press, 1964).
27 Turner Austin, Popkin Margery, J. Susan and Lynette A. Rawlings, *Public Housing and the Legacy of Segregation* (Urban Institute Press, 2008) .
28 Robert Fishman, *Urban Utopias in the Twentieth Century: Ebenezer Howard, Frank Lloyd Wright, Le Corbusier* (Basic Books Inc., Publishers, 1977; 1st ed.).

29 The term originated from the French word for "raw," as Le Corbusier described his choice of material, *béton brut*.

30 https://duckduckgo.com/?q=james+baldwin+negro+removal&t=ffhp&atb=v171-4__&ia=videos&iax=videos.

31 Alfred D. Price, *Urban Renewal: The Case of Buffalo, N.Y.*, 19(3–4) RBPE 125–59 (1991). doi:10.1007/BF02895341; Jon C. Teaford, *Urban Renewal and Its Aftermath, Housing Policy Debate*, 11(2), 443–65 (2000), doi: 10.1080/10511482.2000.9521373; Wendell E. Pritchett, *The Public Menace of Blight: Urban Renewal and the Private Uses of Eminent Domain*, 21 Yale L. & Pol'y Rev. 1 (2003).

32 Kevin Fox Gotham, *A City without Slums: Urban Renewal, Public Housing, and Downtown Revitalization in Kansas City, Missouri*, 60(1) Am. J. Econ. Sociol., Special Issue: City and Country: An Interdisciplinary Collection: 285–316 (2001); Teaford, *Urban Renewal and Its Aftermath*, *supra* note 31.

33 Robert A. Caro, *The Power Broker: Robert Moses and the Fall of New York* (Knopf, 1975).

34 Joseph F. C. DiMento and Cliff Ellis, *Changing Lanes: Visions and Histories of Urban Freeways* (The MIT Press, 2013).

35 Emily Badger and Darla Cameron, How Railroads, Highways and Other Man-made Lines Racially Divide America's Cities, *Washington Post*, Jul. 16, 2015, https://www.washingtonpost.com/news/wonk/wp/2015/07/16/how-railroads-highways-and-other-man-made-lines-racially-divide-americas-cities/?utm_term=.338a6d8f777c.

36 Anthony Foxx, More Than Engineering: Infrastructure Shapes Places, *Urban Institute*, Jan. 16, 2018, https://www.urban.org/infrastructure/more-engineering-infrastructure-shapes-places.

37 https://www1.nyc.gov/site/planning/zoning/background.page.

38 *Village of Euclid v. Ambler Realty Co.*, 272 US 365 (1926).

39 *Arlington Heights v. Metropolitan Housing Dev. Corp.*, 429 US 252 (1977).

40 In *Texas Department of Housing and Community Affairs v. Inclusive Communities Project*, the Supreme Court held that the disparate impact theory applies to housing discrimination claims. This was a significant because the Court had not previously applied the disparate impact theory to housing discrimination cases. 135 S. Ct. 2507. 2015.

41 *Town of Huntington v. NAACP*, 488 US 1023 (1988).

42 *South Burlington NAACP v. Mount Laurel Township*, 67 N.J. 151, 336 A.2d 713, N.J. (1975).

43 Douglas S. Massey, Len Albright, Rebecca Casciano, and Elizabeth Derickson, *Climbing Mount Laurel: The Struggle for Affordable Housing and Social Mobility in an American Suburb* (Princeton University Press, 2013).

44 *Governing* https://www.governing.com/gov-data/education-data/residential-racialsegregation-metro-areas.html.

6

Racial Appeals in Political Campaigns

Political racism can be traced back 150 years to the time of Reconstruction. During that era, the Ku Klux Klan and other hate groups destroyed governments and paved the way for the disenfranchisement, repression, and segregation of the Jim Crow era. In 1968, Richard Nixon and his advisors devised what became known as the "Southern Strategy," which used campaign speeches and commercials to provoke racial resentment.[1]

"Racial resentment" refers to intense, emotionally charged opposition to policies designed to assist racial minorities.[2] Some of the objections are principled and ideological, but for many opponents, there is a strong emotional component. Many who oppose affirmative action believe that employers feel obligated to give jobs to unqualified Blacks and Hispanics. They feel that it allows ill-prepared and undeserving Black students to be admitted to universities at the expense of better-qualified white students. Racial policies designed to promote racial equality are viewed as giving Blacks an unfair and unmerited advantage in employment, college admissions, and government contracting programs.[3] The perception that Blacks are being afforded special treatment breeds racial animosity and ill-will.

Discrimination is viewed by many as a behavioral component of racial prejudice, but it is better understood as an interaction of social cognitions about race and behavioral outlets that bring congruence to a person's racial preferences and social settings.[4] Many of these beliefs are formed during the early childhood years,[5] and they serve as a basis for judgments about events, groups, and ideas during the adult years. Socialized beliefs can provoke negative sentiments when individuals make judgments about issues that activate stereotypes.

Overt racism has diminished in the years since the civil rights laws were enacted.[6] Today, although most whites subscribe to the norm of racial equality, negative stereotypes persist that provoke racial resentment.[7] Racial resentment is different from traditional prejudice because its adherents do not believe that African Americans are biologically inferior. The disposition is not usually overt; it resides deep within an individual's psyche and is related to norms of individual responsibility. This sentiment originates from social dominance, authoritarian orientations, and other personality traits and is often expressed through stereotypes and other biases.

Polling data shows that many whites believe that Blacks lack values such as patriotism, hard work, obeying laws, and refraining from immoral behavior.[8] As the legal barriers to equality were removed decades ago by civil rights laws, some whites believe that the continuing levels of violence and poverty in many minority communities are not attributable to racial discrimination. These conditions, they believe, reflect individuals' failure to take advantage of the opportunities available to them. Many whites also perceive impoverished African Americans as persons who do not value personal responsibility, individualism, hard work, discipline, and self-sacrifice.[9] Fraud and abuse in the welfare system, escalating crime rates, and the dissolution of the traditional family reflect these shortcomings.

Racial resentment can be triggered by unconscious stereotypes that are invoked during the categorization process.[10] "Categorization" is the way in which the brain processes large amounts of information.[11] It operates at a level independent of conscious attitudes, beliefs, and perceptions. This cognitive activity enables individuals to reduce the enormous diversity in the world to a manageable level by aggregating similar concepts in categories.[12]

The Southern Strategy and Racial Resentment

Emotions heavily influence voting decisions.[13] Tali Mendelberg analyzed the effect of implicit racial appeals in campaigns for elective office.[14] She explained that the power of implicit appeals is based on egalitarian norms about race and the continued existence of racial stereotypes and resentments among whites.

Implicit racial appeals avoid any direct references to Black inferiority. They convey a subtle racial message by submerging it in nonracial content. The racial message is usually so subtle that many of its recipients are not aware of the source. Politicians have been able to exploit whites' resentment for decades by using code words that avoid overt references to race. Racial appeals can be very powerful, but they should be subtle enough to avoid an overt violation of the norm of racial equality.

Nixon's code words were, "law and order," "states' rights," and "freedom of choice." His promise to restore "law and order" appealed to white voters in the South and elsewhere who had been alarmed by riots that erupted during the mid-1960s. Nixon opposed the Fair Housing Act and promised to appoint federal judges who would counter the direction that the Supreme Court had taken in *Brown v. Board of Education*. This was the beginning of the Southern realignment in which large numbers of white voters shifted their allegiance from the Democratic Party to the Republican Party. Valentino and Sears attributed this transformation to "symbolic racism," which they defined as a combination of conservatism and racial animosity, rather than explicit racial beliefs.[15]

Welfare Queens and Willie Horton

Ronald Reagan relied heavily on appeals to racial resentment during his campaign. In 1964, three civil rights workers, Andrew Goodman, Michael Schwerner, and James Chaney, disappeared in Neshoba County, Mississippi. They were murdered by local whites enraged by their presence.[16] In 1980, Ronald Reagan chose Neshoba County as the first stop in his election campaign. He told the crowd, "I believe in states' rights." Whites across the country understood what he was saying. "States' rights" was the rhetoric used to resist school desegregation in the South in the 1950s and 1960s.[17] Reagan attacked the legitimacy of food stamps, stating that people at grocery checkout counters were outraged when a "strapping young buck" bought T-bone steaks with food stamps. Race was not mentioned, but the connotation was clear. The "strapping young buck" was a lazy, undeserving African American who was aking advantage of the system.[18]

Reagan's best-known effort to provoke racial resentment was a story about a Chicago "welfare queen" who drove a Cadillac, had eighty aliases, thirty addresses, twelve Social Security cards, and collected benefits for four non-existent deceased husbands, defrauding the government of over $150,000.[19] Race was not mentioned, but the story alluded to the stereotype of a welfare recipient as a dishonest Black woman who was defrauding the system. This exaggerated belief played on whites' stereotypes and resentment about welfare recipients. Reagan's message also took advantage of the strong association of race with poverty.

Lee Atwater, who worked in the Reagan administration in 1981, described the subtle appeals in Reagan's southern strategy in blunt terms:

> You start out in 1954 by saying, "Nigger, nigger, nigger." By 1968 you can't say "nigger"—that hurts you. Backfires. So you say stuff like forced busing, states' rights and all that stuff. You're getting so abstract now [that] you're talking about cutting taxes, and all these things you're talking about are totally economic things and a byproduct of them is [that] blacks get hurt worse than whites . . . [S]itting around saying, "We want to cut this," is much more abstract than even the busing thing, and a hell of a lot more abstract than "Nigger, nigger."[20]

The 1980 election saw the rise of "Reagan Democrats," blue-collar, non-college-educated white voters who abandoned the Democratic Party in the 1970s and 1980s, out of anger at the Democratic Party's support for policies such as welfare and affirmative action.[21] Implicit racial appeals were a powerful means of obtaining votes for Republican presidential candidates.

George H. W. Bush's 1988 campaign used one of the best-known appeals to fear and racial resentment. Willie Horton was convicted of murder and sentenced to life imprisonment. He was granted a weekend leave by the Massachusetts prison furlough program.[22] Horton traveled to Maryland, where he assaulted a white couple, beating the man and raping the woman. He was recaptured and returned to prison.

Bush made repeated references to the Massachusetts furlough program in campaign speeches. Later, a commercial was produced.[23] The narrator stated, "Despite a life sentence, Horton received ten weekend passes from prison.[24] Horton fled, kidnapped a young couple, stabbing the man and repeatedly raping his girlfriend." The words "kidnapping," "stabbing," and "raping" appeared on the screen. The final scene showed a photograph of Dukakis. The words "weekend passes" and "Dukakis on crime" appeared on the screen.[25] A 30-second clip focusing on the consequences of pardons and furloughs seriously damaged Dukakis's political reputation.[26] Horton's race was never mentioned in the narrative, but his image activated the stereotype of a dangerous Black criminal in the minds of white viewers. Overall, Bush's campaign was effective.[27] Dukakis lost the election.[28]

Mitt Romney's Election Strategy

Mitt Romney employed an updated and nationalized version of the Southern Strategy during his campaign.[29] John Judis explained, "[Mitt] Romney's strategy [was] largely a reprise of Ronald Reagan's 1980 election strategy, minus Reagan's public show of amiability and his support among Hispanics. With his recent ads on welfare, Romney is playing on the racial resentments of the white working class the same way Reagan did."[30] A leaked videotape showed Mitt Romney telling wealthy donors at a Boca Raton, Florida, fundraiser that 47 percent of the nation's population do not pay income taxes, believe they are entitled to government assistance, and will never take personal responsibility for their lives.[31] He said:

> There are 47 percent of the people who will vote for the president no matter what. All right, there are 47 percent who are with him, who are dependent upon government, who believe that they are victims, who believe that government has a responsibility to care for them, who believe that they are entitled to health care, to food, to housing, to you name it. That that's an entitlement. And the government should give it to them. And they will vote for this president no matter what. And I mean, the president starts off with 48, 49, 48—he starts off with a huge number. These are people who pay no income tax. Forty-seven percent of Americans pay no income tax. So our message of low taxes doesn't connect. And he'll be out there talking about tax cuts for the rich. I mean that's what they sell every four years. And so my

> job is not to worry about those people—I'll never convince them that they should take personal responsibility and care for their lives. What I have to do is convince the 5 to 10 percent in the center that are independents that are thoughtful, that look at voting one way or the other depending upon in some cases emotion, whether they like the guy or not, what it looks like.[32]

It is not known whether Romney was pandering to wealthy supporters who endorsed this sentiment or whether this was his personal view, but it was seen as a turning point in his campaign.[33]

Romney's election strategy relied heavily on an effort to pit white, middle-class voters against low-income African Americans using coded racial appeals. Many whites perceive poor African Americans as persons who do not value personal responsibility, hard work, and self-sacrifice. Romney's ad alluded to the stereotype of lazy African Americans relying on welfare benefits instead of working to earn a living.[34] Research confirmed that Romney's welfare ad provoked racial resentment.[35]

During the final days of the campaign, Romney resurrected the welfare claim. In the ad, the narrator identifies "gutting" the work requirement in welfare as one of President Barack Obama's "failed" policies in his first term. Citing high unemployment rates and a rise in food stamp recipients, the Romney ad portrays Obama as a threat to future generations. "We may have made it through President Obama's first term," the commercial concluded, as images of white children were shown on the screen, "[i]t's our children who cannot afford a second."[36] The message was "Us, Whites, barely made it through Obama's first term, but our White children cannot afford a second term."

There is a long-standing association in the minds of many white Americans between welfare and "undeserving" African Americans.[37] The image of a welfare recipient in most people's minds is a Black woman.[38] Many whites interpret messages about redistributing wealth from the working middle class to the lazy underclass in highly racialized terms.[39] Code words such as "welfare" and "inner city," especially when combined with racial images, provoke conscious and unconscious racial attitudes that can be decisive in political decision-making.

In the late stages of the race, Romney claimed Obama's "angry and desperate" campaign brought disrespect to the office of the presidency.[40] He said, "Mr. President, take your campaign of division and anger and hate back to Chicago, and let us get about rebuilding and reuniting America."[41] It was Romney who sought to exploit race and class divisions, not Obama.[42]

Romney's campaign messages were intended to reinforce the stereotype that Blacks and Latinos are benefiting at the expense of hardworking whites. The message was that Obama intended to give the undeserving poor government benefits at the expense of hardworking taxpayers. Obama planned to redistribute wealth from the white middle class to the lazy underclass of Blacks and Latinos. This was a dominant theme in Mitt Romney's campaign.

Donald Trump's Presidential Campaigns

On July 16, 2015, Donald Trump announced his candidacy in New York City. The speech was crafted to provoke the maximum effect. Dropping the subtle "dog whistle" tactic of previous campaigns, Trump picked up a megaphone. He called Mexicans "rapists" and criminals who bring drugs across the border. "When Mexico sends its people, they're not sending the best," he said during the announcement. "They're not sending you, they're sending people that have lots of problems and they're bringing those problems. They're bringing drugs, they're bringing crime. They're rapists and some, I assume, are good people, but I speak to border guards and they're telling us what we're getting."

This was a provocative theme that he used throughout his campaigns. In many ways, Trump's election represented a revolt of working-class whites who felt increasingly uneasy about the effects of globalization and a diversifying country in which their standing and political power seemed to be diminishing. Many working-class whites felt that they were not getting their fair share of public resources and decision-making power. These voters were disgusted by the years of gridlock in Washington. They lost faith in the political establishment.

Over the last few decades, communities across the nation have lost factory jobs as a result of the growth of foreign labor markets and advances in technology. America's economy has transitioned from manufacturing and production to the service sectors and high-tech. Trump's message emphasized the many blue-collar jobs that had been outsourced to foreign manufacturers. Trump spoke to the middle-class workers who have been neglected by politicians. He targeted blue-collar workers, focusing on geography and demographics.

Working-class whites in the Midwest were hit hardest by outsourcing and globalization. By attacking government policies, trade, and treaties that contributed to job losses, Trump went after the political establishment. His message was "our government is screwing you." Trump blamed the current conditions on Republican and Democratic elites, the media, and powerful corporations.

Trump held large and raucous rallies throughout his campaigns. Trump's confidence and willingness to be controversial and combative resonated with his supporters. They viewed him as plain-spoken, sincere, and credible. Trump courted working-class whites by promising to restore the manufacturing and industrial economy. He promised to deport immigrants to reduce labor competition for native-born workers.

Researchers have shown that political behavior is driven more by emotions than rational choice. Political orientations are heavily influenced by unconscious emotions. Voters" political reasoning is biased by their subjective sentiments. Negative emotions such as fear and anger drive voting decisions. Trump's bigotry, misogyny, and mistreatment of protesters at his rallies contributed to his appeal. News articles written about his temperament, malignant self-absorption, and poor judgment did not affect his followers.

The unwavering support of Trump's base can be viewed as an act of rebellion. The revolt is as much a rejection of the political establishment as it is active support for Trump. His supporters feel that elites view them with condescension. They feel voiceless and ignored. Trump's promises to build border walls, deport undocumented immigrants, and ban Muslims were welcomed by individuals who were frightened and resentful.

Excessive worry and long-term exposure to stress can distort rational thinking. This can lead to emotional reasoning in which individuals think something is true simply because they feel it is so. Emotional reasoning confuses feelings with facts. This condition impairs intellect and distorts reality. Emotional reasoning emanates in the primitive brain. It is part of the "fight or flight" reaction that helped our ancestors survive dangerous threats. This primitive brain function is provoked by Trump's animosity and fear-inducing rhetoric.

Most voters find it intensely difficult to imagine their least favorite candidate winning an election. Individuals can experience disappointment, worry, fear, sadness, or anger if the candidate they support loses an election. These emotions are very effective in motivating voters. Fear and anxiety are the strongest emotions that drive voting decisions. Anger is a close second. Trump's hyperbolic rhetoric tapped into his audience's anger. Trump discerned the emotional state of his base and capitalized on it. His rhetorical tools were mockery, sarcasm, insults and name-calling.

Fear Mongering: Islamophobia and Immigrants

Islamophobia is an intense and irrational fear of people who practice Islam. Trump focused most of his hateful rhetoric and fear-mongering on Muslims. He was relentless in his claims about the dangers Muslims posed. He appealed to stereotypes of Muslims as dangerous terrorists. Trump used hate, fear, and racism to stir the emotions of white voters. Trump's steady stream of anti-Islam statements was false and inflammatory, but they worked with the voters who became his base. They seemed not to care about Trump's exaggerations and mendacity; all they cared about was the way he made them feel. He was going to "take back America" to the pre-Civil Rights era when white males prevailed. All of these statements were intended to escalate the fears many whites harbored about Muslims. They were stereotyped as potential "terrorists" who pose a risk of harm to Americans. The invocation of fear is a potent means of attracting votes. Trump used it to his advantage.

Immigration is a potent, "make or break," issue for hard-core, conservative Republicans. For voters worried about the decline of America's sovereignty, immigration resonates as an "us-versus-them" issue. These sentiments blame an out-group for deep-seated social and economic anxieties. They are voiced most often by the social and economic classes threatened by outsourcing and new technologies. Concern about Latino immigration has been fed by anxieties about America's status in the world. This is prompted by globalization and growing doubts about the strength of the US economy. The anger is not simply about undocumented immigration; it is more often about Latino immigration. Immigration from Mexico and Central America is viewed by many as contributing to the nation's decline by undermining its national identity.

In *Angry White Men*, Michael Kimball explained how the fears, anxieties, and rage of certain groups have escalated in recent years.[43] Their feelings are caused by dramatic economic, social, and political shifts in the nation. Globalization, deindustrialization, advances in transportation, and developments in technology have transformed America's labor markets. The current pace of change has not been seen since the Industrial Revolution of the late nineteenth and early twentieth centuries when young men and women left family farms and found jobs in the cities of a rapidly industrializing nation. By the mid-1920s, modern American cities were in place. Growth slowed during the Depression of the 1930s. However, defense production for the Second World War in the 1940s ended the depression. Manufacturing escalated dramatically, and jobs grew at an unprecedented pace.

After the war ended, factories that produced trucks and tanks switched to automobiles, lawn mowers, washing machines, and other products for the rapidly growing suburbs. Mortgages insured by the Veterans Administration and Federal Housing Administration financed the creation of thousands of suburban communities across the nation. Suburbanization altered the American landscape. Construction and related industries created unprecedented employment opportunities.

Labor unions negotiated benefits for workers that are now taken for granted. These included the 40-hour work week, overtime compensation, paid vacations, and health insurance. The 1950s were a remarkable time for white, blue-collar males. Competition was limited. There was men's work and women's work, white jobs and Black jobs. Collective bargaining agreements negotiated by unions stated that workers could only be dismissed for good cause shown. A worker could expect to be employed in the same manufacturing plant during his entire career.

Union membership peaked at 35 percent. The male labor participation rate peaked in 1951. The next year, unemployment fell to under 3 percent. Employing, at one time, more than a third of the private workforce, and mostly men without college degrees, manufacturing employment peaked in the summer of 1979 at almost 20 million workers. But by the end of the 1980s recession, that sector had lost almost 3 million jobs. Today, there are about 12 million people working in manufacturing jobs.

Working-class whites have been hit hard by these developments. A large number of white men with only a high school diploma are not working. Many of these men are not only unemployed, but they have also abandoned hope and are not even searching. The white working class is angry about an economy that lost manufacturing and other jobs to low-wage labor markets overseas. They are mad at a government that reached a stalemate in two costly wars and maintained a bureaucracy that did not provide adequate healthcare for veterans. They are fed up with policymakers who bailed out megabanks during the 2008 financial crisis while many lower- and middle-class families lost their homes. Women and minorities now compete for what were "white" jobs a generation ago.

Radio talk-show hosts and outlets such as Fox News pander shamelessly to the anxieties of working-class whites. Fears are stoked by the Islamophobia propagated by right-wing radio hosts and television commentators. In *The Outrage Industry*, the authors examined the influence of conservative talk shows. The inflammatory techniques the hosts use include mockery, sarcasm, insults and name-calling. Some of their claims are out-and-out lies that appeal to paranoia. These are the tactics Donald Trump used during his campaign. There is an echo chamber among media outlets that feed on the fears and anger of middle- and lower-income whites.

For the right-wing media, it is all about revenues. For politicians, it is all about getting re-elected. Working-class whites without college degrees are unaware of the media's profit motives when they vote against their own economic interests. They cannot distinguish their feelings about whiteness from their economic and political well-being.

Conclusion

Middle America is experiencing severe existential angst. The manufacturing jobs that their fathers and grandfathers held are gone. Factories throughout the Northeast and Midwest are shuttered and rusting. Assembly lines that required hundreds of workers are operated by robots. Suicide rates are escalating among working-class whites. Opioid addiction is rampant. Low-wage workers in India and China are producing almost all of the products sold at Walmart and Costco. The service sector is expanding, but the wages and benefits are not what they were for unionized factory jobs.

The high-paying positions available now require higher levels of training and education. In our knowledge economy, a college degree is the minimum requirement for many jobs. This trend has been underway since the 1980s and will not change in the near future. The changes wrought by technological advances will escalate. Trump's promises to bring back manufacturing jobs are as empty as the many false statements that were the cornerstone of his campaign.

Notes

1 See Michael Tonry, *The Social, Psychological, and Political Causes of Racial Disparities in the American Criminal Justice System*, 39 Crime & Just. 273, 300–8 (2010); see generally Jeremy D. Mayer, *Nixon Rides the Backlash to Victory: Racial Politics in the 1968 Presidential Campaign,* 64 Historian 351 (2002) (examining race as the most important domestic issue of Nixon's Presidential Campaign).

2 See generally Donald R. Kinder and Lynn M. Sanders, *Divided by Color: Racial Politics and Democratic Ideals,* 92–127 (The University of Chicago Press, 1996) (discussing the origins and manifestations of racial resentment).

3 See Controversy, *New World Encyclopedia*, http://www.newworldencyclopedia.org/entry/Affirmative_action (last visited Apr. 03, 2013).

4 See James M. Jones, *Prejudice and Racism,* 161–3 (McGraw-Hill, 1972, 2nd ed. 1997).

5 See Jody Armour, *Stereotypes and Prejudice: Helping Legal Decisionmakers Break the Prejudice Habit,* 83 Calif. L. Rev. 733, 741–55 (1995).

6 See generally Howard Schuman et al., *Racial Attitudes in America: Trends and Interpretations*, 99–195 (Harvard University Press, rev. ed. 1997) (discussing trends in white racial attitudes).

7 See Kinder and Sanders, *Divided by Color, supra* note 15. This disposition has been variously labeled "symbolic racism," "modern racism" and "racial resentment." These attitudes include a belief that discrimination does not impose a significant impediment to Black advancement. African Americans should simply work harder to improve their economic and social status. These are slightly different interpretations of the same phenomenon. The more overt forms of prejudice and racism have declined, but negative stereotypes about Blacks persist. See also Patrick. J. Henry and David O. Sears, *The Symbolic Racism 2000 Scale*, 23 Pol. Psychol. 253, 254–8 (2002).

8 Jim Crow on the Down Low, Ware and Wilson.

9 Ware and Wilson, see footnote 8.

10 See Linda H. Krieger, *The Content of Our Categories: A Cognitive Bias Approach to Discrimination and Equal Employment Opportunity*, 47 Stan. L. Rev. 1161, 1187–90 (1995).

11 See generally Linda H. Krieger and Susan T. Fiske, *Behavioral Realism in Employment Discrimination Law: Implicit Bias and Disparate Treatment*, 94 Calif. L. Rev. 997, 1034 (2006) (discussing behavioral theory change in law); Antony Page, *Batson's Blind Spot: Unconscious Stereotyping and the Peremptory Challenge*, 85 B.U. L. Rev. 155, 180–235 (2005) (discussing the processes of categorizing and stereotyping); John L. Jackson, *Racial Paranoia: The Unintended Consequences of Political Correctness*, 81–110 (2008) (discussing the manifestations of racial distrust in American society).

12 See Eleanor Rosch, *Human Categorization,* 1 CCP 1, 1–2 (Neil Warren ed., 1977).

13 See generally Drew Westen, *The Political Brain: The Role of Emotion in Deciding the Fate of the Nation*, 219–48 (Public Affairs, 2008) (discussing Americans conscious and unconscious feelings on race); see also George E. Marcus and Michael B. Mackuen, *Anxiety, Enthusiasm, and the Vote: The Emotional Underpinnings of Learning and Involvement During Presidential Campaigns*, 87 Am. Pol. Sci. Rev. 672, 673–74 (1993).

14 See Tali Mendelberg, *The Race Card: Campaign Strategy, Implicit Messages, and the Norm of Equality* (Princeton University Press, 2001); See also, Leland

Ware and Divid Wilson, *Jim Crow on the "Down Low," Subtle Racial Appeals in Presidential Campaign*, 24 St. John's J. Legal Commentary 299 (2009).

15 See Nicholas A. Valentino and David O. Sears, *Old Times There Are Not Forgotten: Race and Partisan Realignment in the Contemporary South*, 49 Am. J. Pol. Sci. 672, 674 (2005).

16 See Ariel Hart, 41 Years Later, Ex-Klansman Gets 60 Years in Civil Rights Deaths, *New York Times*, Jun. 24, 2005, http://www.nytimes.com/2005/06/24/national/24killen.html?_r=1&oref=slogin.

17 See Jesse Jackson Jr., Reagan: A Legacy of States' Rights, *The Nation*, Jun. 28, 2004, http://www.thenation.com/article/reagan-legacy-states-rights#; see also Lillian Jimenez, *Immigration, Crime, and Neo-Segregation: America's Legacy of Xenophobia: The Curious Origins of Arizona Senate Bill 1070*, 48 Cal. W. L. Rev. 279, 286–87 (2012).

18 See Gertrude Ezorsky, *Racism and Justice: The Case for Affirmative Action* (Cornell University Press, 1991).

19 See David Zucchino, *Myth of the Welfare Queen*, 64–65 (1997). *The New York Times* reported in 1976 Ronald Reagan referred to Linda Taylor, a 47-year-old Chicago welfare recipient, at nearly every stop, stating, "There's a woman in Chicago she has 80 names, 30 addresses, 12 Social Security cards and is collecting veterans' benefits on four nonexisting deceased husbands." See also The Washington Star, "Welfare Queen" Becomes Issue in Reagan Campaign, *N. Y. Times*, Feb. 15, 1976, at 51, http://picofarad.info/misc/welfarequeen.pdf. The real welfare recipient to whom Reagan referred was actually convicted for using two different aliases to collect $8,000.

20 Bob Herbert, Impossible, Ridiculous, Repugnant, *New York Times*, Oct. 6, 2005, http://query.nytimes.com/gst/fullpage.html?res=9C04E6DF1E30F935A35753C1A9639C8B63; Rick Perlstein, Exclusive: Lee Atwater's Infamous 1981 Interview on the Southern Strategy, *The Nation*, Nov. 13, 2012, http://www.thenation.com/article/170841/exclusive-lee-atwaters-infamous-1981-interview-southern-strategy.

21 See generally Stanley B. Greenberg, *Middle Class Dreams: the Politics and Power of the New American Majority*, 23–54 (Yale University Press rev. ed. 1996) (1995) (discussing the symbolism of Macomb County).

22 See George Bush and Willie Horton, *New York Times*, Nov. 4, 1988, http://www.nytimes.com/1988/11/04/opinion/george-bush-and-willie-horton.html.

23 See Willie Horton (National Security PAC, 1988), *Museum of the Moving Image*, http://www.livingroomcandidate.org/commercials/1988/willie-horton (video and transcript available in this link).

24 Ware and Wilson, *supra*.

25 Ware and Wilson, *supra*.

26 See Maggie Haberman, GOP Governors could Face Pardon Issue in 2012 Campaign, *Politico*, May 21, 2011, http://www.politico.com/news/stories/0511/55413.html.

27 See Paul Krugman, Seeking Willie Horton, *New York Times*, Aug. 24, 2007, http://www.nytimes.com/2007/08/24/opinion/24krugman.html?_r=0.

28 Krugman, *supra*.

29 See Karen L. Cox, A New Southern Strategy, *New York Times*, Nov. 17, 2012, http://www.nytimes.com/2012/11/18/opinion/sunday/a-new-southern-strategy.html?pagewanted=1.

30 John Judis, Romney's Losing Strategy, *New Republic*, Aug. 27, 2012), http://www.tnr.com/blog/plank/106587/romney-losing-strategy#.

31 See MoJo News Team, Full Transcript of the Mitt Romney Secret Video, *Mother Jones*, Sep. 19, 2012, 12:00 AM, http://www.motherjones.com/politics/2012/09/full-transcript-mitt-romney-secret-video.

32 Ibid.

33 See Dylan Byers, Jimmy Carter: 47 percent video was "the turning point" for Romney, *Politico*, Dec. 3, 2012, 1:50 PM, http://www.politico.com/blogs/media/2012/12/jimmy-carter-video-was-the-turning-point-for-romney-150914.html.

34 See generally Gilens, *supra* note 76, at 154–73 (discussing racial stereotypes and public responses to poverty).

35 See Michael Tesler, *Testing the Racializing Influence of Romney's Welfare Ad*, YouGov, Aug. 20, 2012, 10:31 AM, http://today.yougov.com/news/2012/08/20/testing-racializing-influence-romneys-welfare-ad/.

36 Michael Tesler, *Testing the Racializing Influence of Romney's Welfare Ad*, YouGov.

37 See generally Gilens, *supra*, at 154–73 (discussing racial stereotypes and public responses to poverty).

38 See Paul Waldman, The Truth about Welfare, *The American Prospect*, Aug. 10, 2012, http://prospect.org/article/truth-about-welfare.

39 Waldman, *supra*.

40 Dan Balz, President Obama, Mitt Romney Running a Most Poisonous Campaign, *Washington Post*, Aug. 15, 2012, http://www.washingtonpost.com/politics/a-most

-poisonous-campaign/2012/08/15/16715a08-e6e7-11e1-8f62-58260e3940a0_story.html.

41 Ware and Wilson, *supra*.

42 Ware and Wilson, *supra*.

43 Michael S. Kimmel, *Angry White Men: American Masculinity at the End of an Era* (Bold Type Books, 2013).

7

Ethnic Minorities in France

Anti-immigrant sentiments are driving the rise of extreme right-wing political parties in France and elsewhere in Western Europe. Immigration from former colonies in North and sub-Saharan Africa has had a significant effect on France's demographic composition. That nation now has the largest Muslim population in Europe. Conflicts involving ethnic minority populations have increased dramatically. In 2004, the French parliament adopted a law that prohibits female students from wearing headscarves in public schools. In 2010, a law was passed that prohibits women from wearing face-covering veils in public places. Both measures have been highly controversial. Many Muslim women interpret their religion to require scarves and veils in public. France's anti-veil laws have, at a minimum, had a discriminatory effect on Muslim women based on their ethnicity, religion, color, and national origin.

Banlieues are low-income, suburban communities. Young *banlieusards* (*banlieue* residents) are stereotyped as gang members, criminals, and potential terrorists. They are otherized as "immigrants" even though many of them are second and third-generation citizens who were born in France. *Banlieusards* are routinely targeted by police who abuse and harass them using identity checks as a pretext. These discriminatory practices treat the young men as second-class citizens and impinge on their rights to freedom of movement and privacy. Police brutality provoked large-scale riots in 1983, the 1990s, and 2005.

Racial and ethnic categories are not officially recognized in France. The French census does not disaggregate data by race or ethnicity. French laws prohibit officials from doing so. France is officially color-blind. Race and ethnicity are important but largely unacknowledged aspects of the immigration debates among French officials. They contend that race does not exist in

France. However, the term "immigrant" has become a shorthand reference to ethnic minorities who are harshly criticized for failing to embrace French values and traditions. This is particularly true in the case of Muslims, as Islam is considered by many to be incompatible with French values. These groups are treated as permanent *étrangeres* unworthy of acceptance by the majority population.

Orientalism

The French perceptions of North Africans are rooted in orientalism, the country's colonial past, and the independence movements of France's former colonies.[1] The expansion of France into Africa and Asia in the nineteenth century was justified on the grounds of *mission civilisatrice* ("civilizing mission"), which was aimed at educating less civilized people in the far reaches of the world.[2] The colonialist rhetoric promoting the civilizing mission appealed to national pride, the glory of French civilization, and the superiority of Christianity over Islam. Jules Ferry, the influential Minister for Public Instruction in the late nineteenth century, was a prominent proponent of the civilizing mission. In a speech made to the French Chamber of Deputies, he said, "Gentlemen, we must speak more loudly and more honestly! We must say openly that indeed the higher races have a right over the lower races. . . . I repeat, that the superior races have a right because they have a duty. They have the duty to civilize the inferior races."[3]

The colonial society established by the French in Africa created two distinct communities: a superior caste consisting of French settlers and an inferior one consisting of Africans.[4] The underlying assumption of the republican model is that immigrants should not be culturally different from white French citizens as they gain citizenship.[5] One of the elements of the assimilation strategy consisted of encouraging Muslim women to stop wearing headscarves.[6] The republican model is premised on a concept of citizenship that rejects the notion of individual differences based on religion, ethnicity, or race. Social integration required indigenous populations to abandon their origins, faith, customs, language.[7] The cultural norms advocated by the republican model consisted of a combination of French language, values, and traditions.

French attitudes about Maghrebis originate from Orientalist stereotypes. In *The Politics of the Veil*, Joan Wallach Scott examined French racism and explained how it is a critical element in the attitudes about immigrants.[8] These attitudes are derived from colonialist traditions and "Orientalism"; ideological biases about cultures in regions designated by Europeans as the Orient.[9] The term "Oriental" in this context denotes generalizations and stereotypes that cross many cultural and national boundaries.[10] It essentializes a prototypical Oriental who is a biologically inferior person who is exotic and culturally backward. A major component of French culture is the conviction that its culture is superior to those of all non-Europeans.[11]

In what many consider to be the canonical text, *Orientalism*, Edward W. Said argued that virtually since the beginning of Western civilization, Europeans have regarded Asian and Middle Eastern people as an alien and threatening "other." Said explained that the version of the Arab world constructed by British and French scholars provided a justification for the colonization of Africa and the Middle East. Eighteenth- and nineteenth centuries European scholars created a condescending and essentialist view of the Arab world not based on any actual knowledge or experience with Arabs. It was the product of their imaginary constructions.

Many of the nineteenth-century Orientalist paintings were propaganda used to support French imperialism. They depicted the East as a place of backwardness, lawlessness, and barbarism tamed by French rule.[12] Antoine-Jean Gros, a painter employed by Napoleon Bonaparte, who never traveled to the Near East himself, conveyed these ideas in paintings featuring Eastern architecture and individuals in exotic dress.[13] Artists such as Eugène Delacroix employed themes of violence and cruelty in their Oriental subjects.[14]

The imagery of Orientalism is suffused with stereotypes of European superiority. Oriental men are depicted as feminine, weak, but dangerous because their hypersexuality poses a threat to white, Western women. Oriental women are depicted as submissive, eager to be dominated and strikingly exotic. The Orient is seen as eccentric, backward, and sensual. European writers describing the Middle East reinforced an image of Arabs and Muslims as uniform, incompetent, and unreflective. This Orient was a creation of the Western imagination.

The Orientalists promoted stereotypes about Arabs, racial inferiority, Islamic fanaticism, and unbridled sexuality, which promoted a caricatured vision of the East. A French study published in 1903 described Algerians as having limited intelligence and being backward and apathetic.[15] It also said that they were undisciplined, dishonest, untrustworthy, and oversexed. For much of the twentieth century, French advertisements, newspaper articles, and novels emphasized the exoticism of North Africans.[16] A consensus emerged about the supposed inferiority and strange customs of North Africans.

During the colonial era and well into the twentieth century, representations of Arab women fell into two predominant stereotypes. One of these consists of prostitutes and women with loose morals. The second is that of the Harem in which multiple women were cloistered and treated as submissive slaves by their husbands. Some of the most popular Orientalist paintings depict harems. Male artists, relying largely on their imaginations, depicted opulently decorated interiors with luxuriant odalisques in the nude or in Oriental dress. Jean-Auguste-Dominique Ingres never traveled to the East but used the harem setting to present an erotic ideal in his voluptuous odalisques.

In French literature, Arab women were depicted in Orientalist fantasies as being driven by their sexual desires. In the early decades of the twentieth century, postcards were circulated in France that depicted Algerian women.[17] Although the photographs purported to be accurate depictions, they were actually posed in a photographer's studio.[18] The photographs were seen as evidence of the exotic and strange customs of Algerians when, in reality, they reflected colonialist fantasies. Arab women have been exoticized and eroticized for the pleasure of European males. The stories and photographs were efforts to peer into Arab women's private spaces. Colonized women were depicted either as morally corrupt, ignorant, and promiscuous individuals who needed the colonizers' guidance. Colonizers used these images to legitimize their colonial administration and to control indigenous women. Orientalist stereotypes of this sort continue to shape French attitudes.

France's Far Right

Immigration has been a potent political issue since the 1980s through, among other things, the influence of the National Front.[19] This far-right political party was founded on October 5, 1972, by activists of the nationalist movement Ordre Nouveau (ex-Occident), attempting an electoral comeback of the French extreme right. Jean-Marie Le Pen was chosen as president of the new movement. He was a former paratrooper and president of the nationalist students' association of Paris.

Since its inception, the National Front has been primarily an anti-immigration party, advocating significant cuts to legal immigration. Its other major policies include opposition to French membership in NATO, the European Union, the Schengen Area, and the eurozone. The party also supports economic interventionism, protectionism, and a zero-tolerance approach to law and order.

Marion Anne Perrine "Marine" Le Pen is the youngest daughter of Jean-Marie Le Pen. She has been president of the party since 2011. Marine Le Pen has led a movement of "de-demonizing" the National Front to soften its image, based on revised positions and expelling controversial members accused of racism and antisemitism. She expelled her father from the party on August 20, 2015, after he made controversial statements about the Holocaust and Vichy France's collaboration with the Nazis during the Second World War. In 2012, she placed third in the presidential election with 17.90 percent of the vote. She launched a second bid to become President of France at the 2017 presidential election. She finished second in the first round of the election, with 21.30 percent of the vote, and faced Emmanuel Macron of the centrist party *En Marche!* in the second round of voting.

On May 7, 2017, she conceded after receiving approximately 33.9 percent of the vote in the second round. The National Rally remains a considerable national force in France. In 2019, it was reported that Le Pen no longer wants France to leave the European Union, nor for it to leave the euro currency. She now hopes to change the EU from the inside along with allied parties. The National Front's agenda consist of racist and xenophobic attacks against immigrants.[20] The party has attracted a significant portion of the French electorate with its demagogic demands to deport Muslim immigrants. A cornerstone of its agenda is the "France for the French" slogan and policies associated with ending further immigration and making it increasingly harder for the foreigners already in France to get their citizenship. Le Pen pledged an immediate end to all immigration and to send all foreigners home. Le Pen consistently related the influx of foreigners to unemployment and crime.

The influence of the National Front on the political agenda is based on its ability to attract voters and to influence voters who support other political parties. This is one of the reasons immigration has remained a hotly contested issue since the 1980s. In April 2002, Le Pen shocked the political establishment when he won 16.9 percent of the vote in the first round of voting in the French presidential election. This left him only three percentage points behind the vote of the incumbent right-wing candidate, Jacques Chirac, who received only 19.9 percent of the vote. The outcome of Le Pen's performance surpassed his 1988 vote.[21]

Conclusion

At some point, France will have to face the reality of an increasingly diverse population. As one researcher explained, "[i]n 1999, France's resident population of foreign or partially foreign origin (immigrants or persons born in France with at least one immigrant parent or grandparent) represented around 13.5 million people, equivalent to between a quarter and a fifth of the total population."[22] The immigration laws fail to recognize the nation's current demographic composition. The government has made continuous efforts to keep North and sub-Saharan immigrants out while failing to address the needs of French nationals with African ancestry.

Notes

1 Quentin Duroy, *North African Identity and Racial Discrimination in France: A Socioeconomic Analysis of Capability Deprivation*, 307 Rev. Soc. Eco. 315–316 (2011).

2 Ibid; Ellen Wiles, *Headscarves, Human Rights, and Harmonious Multicultural Society: Implications of the French Ban for Interpretations of Equality*, 41 Law & Soc'y Rev. 699, 704 (2007).

3 Jules François Camille Ferry, Speech Before the French Chamber of Deputies, Mar. 28, 1884, *Modern History Sourcebook: Jules Ferry (1832–1893): On French Colonial Expansion,* http://www.fordham.edu/halsall/mod/1884ferry.asp.

4 Duroy, *North African Identity and Racial Discrimination in France, supra.*

5 Duroy, *North African Identity and Racial Discrimination in France, supra*; *The Color of Liberty: Histories of Race in France* (Sue Peabody and Tyler Stovall, eds., Duke University Press, 2003); Albert Memmi, *The Colonizer and the Colonized* (Beacon Press, 1957).

6 Wiles, *Headscarves, Human Rights, and Harmonious Multicultural Society, supra.*

7 Duroy, *North African Identity and Racial Discrimination in France, supra.*

8 Joan Wallach Scott, *The Politics of the Veil* (Princeton University Press, 2007).

9 Edward W. Said, *Orientalism* (Vintage Books, 1979); Edward W. Said, *Culture and Imperialism* (Vintage Books, 1994).

10 "Orientalism" was originally a term used by art historians and other scholars to categorize depictions of Middle Eastern and East Asian cultures by artists and writers from the West. Christine Peltre, *Orientalism in Art* (Abbeville Press, 2005).

11 Said, Orientalism, *supra* at 39. See also *Matthew Olmsted Are Things Falling Apart? Rethinking the Purpose and Function of International Law*, 27 Loy. L.A. Int'l & Comp. L. Rev. 401, 423 (2005); William Lafi Youmans, *Edward Said and Legal Scholarship*, 3 UCLA J. Islamic & Near E.L. 107 (2003–2004); Frantz Fanon, *A Dying Colonialism* (1965).

12 Todd Porterfield, *The Allure of Empire: Art in the Service of French Imperialism 1798–1836*, 132–133 (1998); Orientalism in Nineteenth-Century Art, *The Metropolitan Museum of Art, Heilbrun Timeline of Art History*, http://www.metmuseum.org/toah/hd/euor/hd_euor.htm.

13 Porterfield, *The Allure of Empire, supra.*

14 Laurel Ma, *The Real and Imaginary Harem: Assessing Delacroix's Women of Algiers as an Imperialist Apparatus*,19 Penn Hist. Rev., Issue 1, 9–18 (2011).

15 Scott, *Politics of the Veil, supra.*

16 Dana S. Hale, *French Images of Race on Product Trademarks During the Third Republic, The Color of Liberty, Histories of Race in France, supra*, 131–46.

17 Scott, *Politics of the Veil, supra*; Malek Alloula, *The Colonial Harem*, 3–7 (1986) See also *French Orientalism: Culture, Politics and the Imagined Other* (Desmond Hosford and Chong J. Wojtkowski, eds., 2010).

18 Scott, *Politics of the Veil, supra.*

19 Paul Hainsworth, *The Extreme Right in France: The Rise and Rise of Jean-Marie Le Pen's front National*, 40(2) Representation 101–14 (2004).

20 Mustafa Dikec, *Badlands of the Republic: Space, Politics and Urban Policy,* 56–60 (Blackwell Press, 2007).

21 Historically, Voters Don't Follow the Front National's Advice, *LeFigaro*, Apr. 26, 2012, http://plus.lefigaro.fr/note/historically-voters-dont-follow-the-front-nationals-advice-20120426–905492.

22 Michéle Tribalat, *An Estimation of the Foreign-Origin Populations of France in 1999*, 59(1) Population-E 49–80 (2004).

8

Nationalism, Nativism, and the New Right

Introduction

This chapter examines the growing influence of ethnic nationalism in the American and European political spheres. Ethnic nationalism refers to belonging to a group defined by ethnic identity, language, religion, and similar traits. In the eighteenth and nineteenth centuries, European nationalism was a unifying force that brought people of diverse backgrounds together by subordinating their ethnic identities to a territorial unit dominated by a secular state.[1]

In the late twentieth and early twenty-first centuries, ethnic nationalism reemerged in Western Europe. In France, Germany, Austria, the Scandinavian countries, and elsewhere in Europe, candidates running on ethnic nationalist platforms have made significant inroads in governing bodies. Brexit was fueled, in part, by anti-immigrant sentiments.

The influx of ethnic minority immigrants from North Africa, Asia, and the Middle East is one of the main reasons for the rise of far-right parties. Native populations are motivated by a desire to preserve their homelands from what they view as the corrosive effects of globalization and migration. The central theme of ethnic nationalists is that nations are defined by a shared heritage, a common language, a common faith, and a shared ethnic ancestry.

Populism is another aspect of anti-immigrant sentiment.[2] Populists view society as divided into two antagonistic groups: the "common" people and "the corrupt elite." The elite is viewed as a parasitical class that enriches itself while ignoring ordinary people's grievances. The immoral values of the elite contrast with the wisdom and common sense of the regular people. Exclusionary populism seeks to exclude certain groups from "the people" and limit their access to the same benefits and rights as others. Nativism combines nationalism with xenophobia, saying states should be limited to members of the native group; non-native elements are viewed as fundamentally threatening.

Many anti-immigrant groups subscribe to the "Replacement" theory.[3] This is a white nationalist, far-right conspiracy theory which states that with the complicity of elites, the white European population is being progressively replaced by non-European peoples. Specifically, Arab and sub-Saharan Muslim populations from Africa and the Middle East are being replaced through mass migration, demographic growth, and a drop in European birth rates.

The replacement theory creates a dangerous dynamic in which believers view immigrants and non-white citizens as an existential threat to their communities.[4] The theory has led to violent outbursts such as the murder of fifty-one people at the Al Noor mosque and Linwood Islamic Center in Christchurch, New Zealand,[5] and the killing of more than twenty mostly Hispanic shoppers in El Paso, Texas.[6]

Globalization, deindustrialization, and technological advances dramatically transformed the labor markets, reducing the need for workers. The rising number of ethnic minority immigrants began to be seen as an economic, social, and cultural threat to native populations. This is reflected in political developments over two decades in France, Germany, Austria, the Netherlands, and Belgium. Other political parties in Europe, including Sweden, Denmark, Norway, Finland, and Italy, are analyzed as additional examples of the rise of the radical right.[7]

Germany

Alternative for Germany (AfD) was established in 2013 by a group of conservatives, many of whom had been members of the Christian Democratic Union, the center-right party that German Chancellor Angela Merkel leads. They were frustrated with what they saw as a shift to the center on a range of policies, including Merkel's decision to commit German taxpayer funds to bail out Greece.

The AfD is a radical, right-wing political party that shares an ideology similar to France's far-right National Front, Austria's far-right Freedom Party, the populist, anti-Islam Dutch Freedom Party led by Geert Wilders, and the UK's anti-EU party, Ukip. In 2017, when the AfD entered Germany's Parliament it was the first time a far-right party had done so in seven decades.[8]

Representing the far-right faction of the AfD is 76-year-old Alexander Gauland, a lawyer and journalist who was a former member of the CDU.[9] An example of the moderate wing of the AfD faction is 38-year-old economist Alice Weidel, who lives in Switzerland with her female partner who comes from Sri Lanka.[10] In 2015, after nearly 1 million migrants arrived in Germany seeking asylum, the AfD shifted its focus to domestic security and immigration. The party's tone became increasingly nationalistic, populist, and, in some cases, racist.

In view of the horrors of the Second World War, Hitler, and the Holocaust, Germany is cautious about hate groups. The country places strict limits on speech and expression when it comes to right-wing extremism. It is illegal to produce, distribute, or display symbols of the Nazi era, such as swastikas and the Hitler salute, along with many symbols that neo-Nazis developed as proxies to get around the law. Holocaust denial is also illegal. There is the legal concept of "Volksverhetzung," the incitement to hatred: anyone who denigrates an individual or a group based on their ethnicity or religion, or anyone who tries to rouse hatred or promote violence against such a group or an individual, could face a sentence of up to five years in prison.[11]

AfD members have urged Germany to rethink its national culture of atonement and remembrance of Nazi crimes.[12] The AfD promised to restore law and order and a sense of national pride. The party also promised to increase border security, push back against further European Union integration, and to oppose the use of German taxpayer money to bail out foreign banks. The AfD wants to revamp Germany's pension system, cutting a government program that rewards private pension savers.

The party is anti-Islamic, rejecting inclusive language used by Ms. Merkel and past leaders, stating that a religion that does not respect the constitution and laws of the country is not compatible with German democracy. The AfD fights against Germany's "memory culture," calling for an end to apologizing for the past. The AfD wants to close the EU's borders, institute rigorous identity checks along Germany's national borders, and set up holding camps abroad to prevent migrants from moving to Germany. Although nominally favoring a targeted immigration policy along the Canadian model, Alice Weidel has said the party wants to achieve "negative immigration" to Germany. She also complains that Germany is being "Islamified."

Austria's Freedom Party

On March 12, 1938, German troops, accompanied by Adolf Hitler, entered Austria. A Nazi government in Austria was established. It collaborated with Hitler in proclaiming the Anschluss on March 13, 1938. Pictures of Hitler entering Vienna in 1938 show cheering crowds. A large portion of the Austrian population was very pleased with the unification of the two countries. In Austria, anti-Semitism was more deeply rooted than in Germany. Once Austria became part of the Third Reich, it disappeared as a country and became a new province of Germany, called Ostmark. Austria was completely absorbed into Germany.

During the Second World War, hundreds of thousands of Austrians fought as German soldiers. A substantial number of them served in the SS, the elite military corps of the Nazi Party. While many Austrians were not Nazis, popular support for Germany's wartime policies remained strong until the later phases of the war.[13]

The Austrian Freedom Party (FPO) was founded in 1956 by a group of former Nazis.[14] Its first chairman was a former SS general, and most of its rank and file were former Nazi party members. The FPO became a European-style liberal party, but under the leadership of Jörg Haider, it evolved into a far-right, populist party. Under Haider's leadership, the FPO increased electoral gains in parliamentary elections, going from five percent in 1983 to 26.9 percent 1999.[15] The charismatic Haider transformed the party, increasing its popular appeal.[16]

Throughout his career, Haider vigorously opposed immigration and Islam. The FPO moved to the right, reflecting Haider's nationalist, anti-immigration, and anti-EU views.[17] In the 1990s, the FPO focused on resisting immigrants with Turkish, Yugoslav, and African backgrounds. Haider became internationally known for his provocative, pro-Nazi statements and praise of Adolf Hitler's policies. He was most notorious for a series of outrageous statements, including praising the Waffen-SS and the employment policies of the Nazi government. In remarks made to a group of Austrian veterans of the Second World War, Haider said the Waffen-SS deserved "honor and respect."[18]

The Freedom Party focused its efforts on expanding its constituency. By 2005, the FPO had positioned itself as the most right-wing and anti-establishment party in Austria. The party focused on patriotism and the defense of American culture and tradition. It is a populist party voicing the protest of "outsiders" against "insiders," of "have-nots" against "haves," and "modernization losers" against "modernization winners." The FPO is a right-wing party. Xenophobic and racist attitudes play a significant role in its outlook. It supported the denial of social benefits to immigrants. The FPO contends that immigrants threaten to reduce the resources available to poorer Austrians. Immigrants are considered a security risk to the local population. They are seen by the FPO as a threat to Austrian identity and culture.[19]

The FPO promoted identity politics centered on the exclusion of the ethnic "other." The Islam Act of 1912 states that Muslims were free to "show their religion in public, administer their internal affairs autonomously, and establish foundations for religious, educational, and charitable purposes.[20] When the Islamic Religious Community was recognized as a representative body for all Muslims in Austria, Muslims were given the same rights as other legally recognized churches and denominations.

Currently, there is only one member of parliament with a Muslim background, while at the regional level, there are few Muslims in political office. The Islam Act of 2015, which is partly aimed at tackling Islamist radicalism, gives Muslims more legal security but bans foreign funding for mosques and imams. In 2017, the Austrian government implemented another law which banned facial veiling.[21] Haider resigned his leadership of the FPO in late February 2000. His final split with the FPO occurred when he announced that he was forming a new party, the Alliance for the Future of Austria.

On October 11, 2008, however, Haider died from injuries sustained in a car accident.[22] After a string of leaders following Haider's death, Heinz-Christian Strache was elected FPO party chairman in 2005. He led the party further to the right on an anti-immigrant and anti-foreigner platform. Strache was forced to resign after a video sting. A scandal erupted when footage from a 2017 meeting was published in the German media, showing Strache and another FPO official proposing to offer government contracts to a supposed Russian oligarch's niece.[23] The party has been led by Norbert Hofer since September 2019.

Belgium

Belgium is a sovereign, constitutional monarchy with a parliamentary system. Its institutional organization is complex and structured on regional and linguistic grounds. The nation is divided into three autonomous regions: the Flemish Region in the north, Wallonia in the south, and the Brussels-Capital Region. Prior to 1970, Belgium was a unitary state. An unwritten rule prevailed that, except for the prime_minister, the government had to include as many Flemish as French-speaking ministers. Tensions that had been building throughout the twentieth century between the two linguistic groups led to major administrative restructuring during the 1970s, '80s, and '90s.[24]

A series of constitutional reforms dismantled the unitary state, culminating in an agreement which laid the groundwork for the establishment of the federal state. This was approved by the parliament in July 1993 and incorporated into a new constitution in 1994. National authorities now share power with executive and legislative bodies representing the major politically defined regions of Belgium. These include the Flemish Region (Flanders), the Walloon Region (Wallonia), and the Brussels-Capital Region. Communal and provincial elections take place every six years, regional and community council elections occur every five years, and national elections are held at least every five years.[25]

Belgium's leading political parties were historically divided into French and Flemish-speaking factions. However, as the country moved toward a federal system, the differences between these wings became more pronounced. The traditional political parties include the Social Christians, the Flemish Christian Democrats and their French counterpart, the Humanist and Democratic Center; the Socialist Party divided into Flemish- and French-speaking branches; the Flemish Liberals and Democrats; and the French-speaking Reform Movement. Other ethnic and special-interest parties include

French- and Flemish-speaking Green parties, Flemish separatist parties, and the right-wing National Front in Wallonia.[26]

The ideology of one party, Vlaams Blok, started out with its radical nationalist rejection of the People's Union compromise on the Flemish autonomy issue and later increasingly focused on immigration, security, and the defense of traditional values. Nationalism, the main issue for the party, is based on the idea that an ethnic community is a naturally occurring entity whose cultural, material, ethical, and intellectual interests need to be preserved. Immigration became an important issue in the late 1980s. In 1992, the party issued a 70-point plan, which included proposals to stop all immigration, return most immigrants to their native countries by force, and legally discriminate against resident migrants in labor, housing, and education. Immigrants were considered a threat to the Flemish ethnic community. Concerns about crime and security were also linked to immigration.[27] The party blamed Turks and Moroccans for various criminal activities and sought a zero-tolerance approach regarding law and order.

In October 2000, the Centre for Equal Opportunities and Opposition to Racism, together with the Dutch-speaking Human Rights League in Belgium, filed a complaint in a local court in which they claimed that organizations connected to the Vlaams violated a 1981 anti-racism law. After losses in lower courts on technicalities, the Belgian court of appeals ruled in April 2004 that some of the party's organizations breached the anti-racism law and that the party sanctioned discrimination. The ruling meant that the party would lose access to state funding and access to television, effectively shutting the party down.[28]

The party subsequently reorganized itself as the Vlaams Belang. The Vlaams Belang, a party with a strong anti-immigrant policy, had electoral successes in Flanders in the late 1990s and early 2000s. By 2004, the party became the single most popular Flemish party in Belgium, supported by about one in four voters in the Flemish electorate.[29]

Geert Wilders and the Party for Freedom in the Netherlands

Geert Wilders is a Dutch businessman and politician. He was born in 1963, the youngest of four children. His father was a printing company executive. He was raised in Venlo, a staunchly Roman Catholic town in the disadvantaged southern province of Limburg, but he never embraced religion. Wilders has been the Leader of the Party for Freedom (PVV) that he founded in 2006. The PVV is the only party in the history of the Dutch parliament to lack a membership base. The party has had just one member, Geert Wilders. He is the parliamentary leader of his party in the House of Representatives.

Wilders is best known for his criticism of Islam and the EU. The PVV has proposed banning the Koran and shutting down all mosques in the Netherlands. The party is populist, nativist, Eurosceptic, and since 2012, it has advocated withdrawal from the EU.[30] In the decade since the Freedom Party won its first parliamentary seats in 2006, Wilders has reshaped the politics of the Netherlands. As an article in Politico noted, "Policy debates, media attitudes, party landscape all have been affected by Wilders' politics."[31]

Debates in the Netherlands on immigration have concentrated on non-Western Muslims, especially those of Turkish and Moroccan origin. About six percent of the current population in the Netherlands is estimated to be Muslim.[32] A fierce debate erupted after the murder, in broad daylight, of Theo van Gogh on November 2, 2004, by a Dutch-Moroccan, Mohammed Bouyeri. The killer impaled a five-page letter in van Gogh's chest with a knife. The crime was triggered by the broadcast of van Gogh's and Ayaan Hirsi Ali's movie, Submission, in which they criticized Islam and the subordinate status of Muslim women.[33] Soon after the murder, which stirred a fierce debate about the integration of Muslims in Dutch society, it was learned that Wilders was on the "death list" of Bouyeri's sympathizers. Since then, Wilders has slept in safe houses and lives under strict, round-the-clock police protection.

In the 1960s and 1970s, the Netherlands had a reputation as a liberal, progressive, and tolerant society, a supporter of the United Nations and a generous donor of development aid. Pim Fortuyn was the first Dutch politician to make Islam a central element of his electoral agenda. The openly homosexual former sociology professor's controversial opinions gained credibility after the 9/11 attacks, when the integration of Muslims became a widely discussed topic in the Netherlands. On May 6, 2002, however, Fortuyn was assassinated by an environmental activist a few days before the Dutch general election.[34] Geert Wilders' party emerged as its successor.[35]

Fitnah is a 2008 film by Geert Wilders. The seventeen-minute film argues that the Quran motivates its followers to hate anyone who violates Islamic teachings. The film is a mixture of images from 9/11, the Madrid bombings, and words from the Quran. Wilders was temporarily banned from entering Britain after it aired. He was prosecuted under Dutch hate-speech laws for "group insult" and "incitement" of "hatred" and "discrimination," but was eventually acquitted. In 2012, he wrote a book, Marked for Dead: Islam's War Against the West and Me.[36] In December 2016, Wilders was found guilty of inciting discrimination and insulting a group, but he was acquitted of inciting hate. Death threats are part of Wilders' daily life because of his strident anti-Islam rhetoric. Since assuming office, Wilders has warned of the so-called "Islamization of the Netherlands." In addition to professing his "hate" for Islam, he has compared the Quran to Adolph Hitler's Mein Kampf.[37]

A 2017 study examined Wilders' supporters. Most PVV supporters in the sample did not have a university degree. The share with a university degree is less than a fifth and considerably lower compared to the share of university-educated individuals among supporters of other parties. PVV supporters displayed much more anti-foreigner and anti-globalization sentiment and higher levels of political distrust compared to supporters of other parties. The survey showed 87.2 percent of PVV supporters think that there are too many foreigners in the Netherlands and 80.7 percent view political elites as generally untrustworthy. Anti-globalization sentiment is the most pronounced among PVV supporters compared to those of other parties. PVV supporters are less likely to have a university degree, display higher levels of anti-foreigner sentiment, are more likely to distrust political elites, and they are much more Eurosceptic than other voters.[38]

Italy's Northern League

Italy is a parliamentary republic with a multi-party system. It has been a democratic republic since June 2, 1946, when the monarchy was abolished by popular referendum and a constituent assembly was elected to draft a constitution, which was promulgated on January 1, 1948. From the end of the Second World War until the 1990s, Italy had two dominant parties, the

Christian Democratic Party and the Italian Communist Party, along with several small but influential parties. Currently, the major parties include the Five Star Movement, the League, the Democratic Party, and Italy Alive.

The Northern League was established in 1991 by Umberto Bossi as a federation of six regional parties in north and north-central Italy.[39] It was led by Roberto Maroni until 2013. It is a federalist and fiscal-reform movement with large support in Italy's northern regions. The League wants more power for Italy's regions, especially those in the North. The party's constitution states that its goal is fiscal federalism, under which the regions that make up northern areas would keep tax revenues generated there. The party's ideology is a combination of political federalism, fiscal federalism, regionalism, and defense of northern Italian traditions. It has advocated the secession of the North. The League has maintained an anti-southern Italian position, often stereotyping southern Italians as welfare abusers, criminals.[40]

Matteo Salvini joined the Movement of Padanian Communists and worked as a journalist for the La Padania newspaper. At age twenty, he was elected to the Milan city council. Salvini was elected as a Northern League deputy to the European Parliament in 2004, 2009, and 2014, and to the Italian Chamber of Deputies in 2008. In 1990, Salvini became a member of the northern League.[41] Northern League is regarded as a right-wing, populist party. Removing "Northern" from the League's brand was an effort to expand its base and connect with central and southern Italian voters.

Salvini served as Deputy Prime Minister of Italy and Minister of the Interior from June 1, 2018, to September 5, 2019. He has been a Senator in the Italian Senate since March 2018. On December 7, 2013, Salvini defeated Umberto Bossi with 82 percent of the vote. A week later, his election was ratified by the party's federal congress. Under Salvini's leadership, the party has shifted increasingly to the far right on issues such as crime and immigration. Salvini is seen as a hardline Eurosceptic politician, with a critical view of the European Union and the euro. He opposes illegal immigration into Italy as well as the EU's management of asylum seekers.

Among the League's policies announced during the 2018 election campaign were a flat tax at 15 percent; legalization and taxation of prostitution; free, state-funded daycare; rejection of a bill that would grant Italian citizenship to those born and educated in Italy with foreign parents; and tighter controls on immigration. In general elections, the party's result was 10.1 percent in 1996. That figure dropped to 8.3 percent in 2008, then 4.1 percent in 2013. In the 2018 elections, the League became the third largest political party with 17.69 percent. In the 2019 EU elections, it placed first with 34.26 percent of the votes.

In 2015 and 2016, more than 1 million refugees made their way to the European Union, the largest number of them originating from Syria. Since then, refugee arrivals have continued, although at a much slower pace and involving people from a wider range of countries in Africa, Asia, and the Middle East. By the end of 2016, nearly 5.2 million refugees and migrants reached European shores.[42] Thousands lost their lives or have gone missing since 2015. In 2018, more than 138,000 people risked their lives trying to reach Europe by sea. More than 2,000 of them drowned.

Under the Common European Asylum System, international protection is granted to those migrants who qualify as refugees due to a well-founded fear of persecution. Subsidiary protection status is granted to those who would face a real risk of suffering serious harm if returned to his/her country of origin. Member states are required to return illegal economic migrants to their country of origin.[43]

One of Salvini's first moves after he took office in 2018 was to declare Italian ports closed to ships rescuing people fleeing Libya by boat.[44] Later there were twenty-five standoffs between rescue vessels and Italian authorities.[45] In 2019, Salvini prevented 116 migrants from disembarking from a coastguard ship in the Mediterranean. Prosecutors in the southern Sicilian city of Catania accused Salvini of kidnapping and abuse of power.[46] He faces up to fifteen years in jail for aggravated kidnapping. In February 2020, the Italian Senate formally authorized criminal proceedings. If Salvini is convicted and sentenced to a term of more than two years, he could be barred from holding public office for six years, preventing him from running for prime minister at the next election in 2023. Salvini was ousted from power in 2019 during the formation of a new coalition government between the Five Star Movement and the center-left Democratic Society.[47]

Norway's Progress Party

The Progress Party (FrP)[48] is considered the most right-wing party to be represented in a national parliament. It is currently Norway's third largest political party, with twenty-six representatives in the general assembly. It is among the most successful right-wing populist parties in Europe. It is a neoliberal economic party and has never been as far-right as the National Front National in France or the AfD in Germany. The Progress Party was founded as a libertarian, anti-bureaucracy, and anti-establishment party.[49] The party advocates for a strict and responsible immigration policy, stating that the number of immigrants and refugees admitted to Norway should be drastically decreased.[50] The FrP also contends that Norway needs to rethink its immigration policies.

Norway follows the Nordic model of social welfare.[51] Compulsory membership in a national health insurance system guarantees all Norwegians free medical care in hospitals, compensation for doctors' fees, and free medicine, and an allowance to compensate for lost wages. Membership fees securing cash benefits during illness or pregnancy, covered by another insurance fund, are compulsory for salaried employees and optional for the self-employed.

A pension system ensures citizens upon retirement a standard of living reasonably close to the level that the individual had achieved during his or her working life. The pension covers old age and cases of disability or loss of support. The premiums are paid by the individual members, employers, municipalities, and the state. The Progress Party supports the system.

The FrP advocates tightened rules for claiming asylum and on refugees or immigrants bringing family members to Norway. It supported a ban on burqas in nurseries, schools, universities, and public spaces. The FrP argues that elements of Islam are incompatible with Norwegian society. The Progress Party entered a governing coalition for the first time following the parliamentary elections of 2013.[52] The party holds anti-establishment, anti-immigration, and strict law and order positions. Most of the party's delegates view immigration as a serious threat to Norway's national identity.

Norway's right-wing Progress Party resigned from the governing coalition after a decision to bring home from Syria a woman suspected of affiliation with the Islamic State group and her two children.[53] The woman and her family returned to Norway in January 2020.

Sweden Democrats

The ruling party in Sweden is the Social Democrats, which has been in power for most of the twentieth century. The second largest party is the Moderates, a center-right party and the main opposition to the Social Democrats. They support free market principles, economic liberalism, and tax cuts. Since 2014, the Sweden Democrats have been the third largest party in parliament. It is a populist, nationalistic, xenophobic, Islamophobic, and far-right party that advocates for "ordinary people" against a corrupt elite.[54]

Sweden has long been a beacon of tolerance. In the 1930s, the Social Democrats were responsible for setting up much of Sweden's social welfare system. It includes, among other things, subsidized physician care; free public hospital treatment; subsidized dental care; subsidized prescription drugs; free abortions; free maternity clinics for prenatal care; cash benefits to compensate for loss of wages due to sickness; monthly payments to parents for each child; paid leave to care for each child up to first year in school; subsidized child care; unemployment insurance; pensions for retired persons; disability pensions; and surviving spouse and orphan pensions.[55]

The Sweden Democrats were founded in 1988. Jimmie Akesson has been party leader since 2005. The party has roots in Swedish fascism and white nationalism but began distancing itself from its past during the late 1990s and early 2000s.[56] Under Akesson's leadership, the SD underwent a process of reform by expelling extremist members and rejecting fascism and Nazism. In the 2018 national elections, the Sweden Democrats gained thirteen seats for a total of 62.[57]

The party now espouses a doctrine of cultural nationalism, saying it welcomes foreigners who learn Swedish and accept the culture. The party opposes multiculturalism. The SD accuses the traditional centrist parties of undermining social welfare by encouraging the immigration of Muslims who, they argue, do not share Swedish values.[58]

Globalization, deindustrialization, spending cutbacks, rising unemployment, and the violent breakup of Yugoslavia in 1991–2 caused an influx of refugees during those years. In 2015, there was a large increase in the number of migrants and refugees traveling to Europe from areas across the Mediterranean or overland through eastern Europe. During the "Immigrant Crisis," more than one million people crossed into Europe.[59] They embarked on dangerous journeys to escape conflicts and find a better life.

The sudden influx of migrants sparked a crisis as Europe struggled to respond. Thousands died attempting to reach its shores. While some countries welcomed the migrants, others erected fences and closed their borders. "Sweden is full. Don't come to us! We can't give you more money or provide any housing." This was the message in English on leaflets handed out by Jimmie Akesson in the Turkish town of Edirne, which is close to the borders of Greece and Bulgaria.[60] The Sweden Democrats were Eurosceptic, but they have reversed their policy of calling for the country to follow Britain out of the EU. Citing uncertainty over Brexit, party leader Jimmie Akesson said the Sweden Democrats, which have long advocated a vote on a so-called "Swexit," now hoped to change the EU from within.[61]

Support for the Sweden Democrats has grown since the 1990s. The party crossed the 4 percent threshold necessary for parliamentary representation for the first time during the 2010 general election, polling 5.7 percent and gaining twenty seats in the national legislature. The party received increased support in the 2018 general election, when it polled at 17.5 percent and secured sixty-two seats in parliament, making it the third largest party in Sweden.

Denmark

The system of governance in Denmark is a parliamentary democracy. The Parliament is called the *Folketing*, and it has a multi-party structure. Since no single party has enough of the 179 votes to rule on its own, several parties negotiate on goals to form a multi-party coalition. The leading figure of one of the stronger parties in that coalition becomes the prime minister, while leaders from the other coalition parties can take on important roles such as the Minister for Justice, the Minister for Finance, and the Minister for Foreign Affairs.[62]

The four oldest and most influential parties are the Conservative People's Party, the Social Democrats, Venstre, and Social Liberal Party. The government typically consists of a major party in coalition with several smaller parties. No party has won an outright majority since the beginning of the twentieth century. Since then, the country has been ruled by coalitions among two or more parties.

The Danish People's Party (DPP) was established in 1995. It is a nativist, populist, and right-wing organization that opposes immigration and membership in the EU.[63] In 2014, the party won the European Parliament election with 27 percent of the vote. The DPP received 21 percent of the vote in the 2015 general election, which made it the second largest party in Denmark.[64]

In mid-February 2015, Copenhagen was shaken by a pair of terrorist attacks that occurred within hours of each other. A filmmaker was killed, and three policemen were wounded when a gunman shot through the windows of a cultural center, which was hosting a panel discussion titled "Art, Blasphemy and Freedom of Expression" that included the participation of a Swedish artist whose published depiction of the Prophet Muhammad in 2007 had stirred controversy and had made him the target of previous attacks.[65]

Although Denmark did not receive as many migrants and refugees as some other European countries, the migrant crisis of 2015–16 had a significant impact. In January 2016, Denmark tightened its borders by imposing identity checks on everyone entering the country. Face covering was banned in public, and benefits were reduced for asylum seekers.[66] A cornerstone of the Danish welfare system is free and equal rights to benefits such as healthcare and education for all citizens. The Danish welfare model also plays an important role in balancing work and family life. Parents are entitled to fifty-two weeks of leave with a maternity subsistence allowance. Free education for all is a key priority in Denmark. Higher education has a long tradition of cooperation with business, industry, and research institutes.[67]

The center-right government, with support from the Danish People's Party, pushed Denmark's immigration policies to the right.[68] Denmark has some of the most aggressive anti-immigrant policies in Europe.[69] That has included taking out foreign newspaper advertisements warning potential migrants that they are not welcome. It also authorized police to seize cash and valuables from arriving asylum seekers to offset the cost of their maintenance.[70]

Social Democrats coopted the DPP by adopting their stance on immigration. In 2015, right-wing parties suffered major losses, with the DPP experiencing the largest defeat, losing more than half of their seats in Parliament. The DPP's share of the vote fell from 21.1 percent to 8.7 percent. Mainstream parties coopted key aspects of the radical right's platform. The governing liberal conservative party, Venstre, and the main opposition party, the Social Democrats, voted in favor of even stricter immigration policies.

Two new radical competitors successfully challenged the DPP. The New Right, which was founded in 2015, is more nativist and much more economically right-wing than the DPP. Another party, Hard Line, emerged more recently and is largely a media-created Islamophobic, single-issue party.[71] The party wants to deport most of the Muslim population in Denmark. Climate and welfare were the main issues for Danish voters during this election, with immigration coming in third place.

The Finns Party

Finland allied itself with Nazi Germany during the Second World War to win back territories lost to the USSR during the winter war of 1939–40. The peace treaty that ended the war in March 1940 left Finnish independence intact. Joining the Nazi attack on the USSR endangered Finland's national existence and cost tens of thousands of lives. In 1944–5 the Red Army could have occupied Finland, but Stalin chose not to, mainly because Finnish leaders admitted their error and pledged neutrality and friendship with the Soviet Union. "Finlandization," as it was called, enabled Finland to remain free of Soviet domination and communist takeover.[72]

Finland's GDP per capita is among the highest in the world, allowing the country to offer a high living standard. The distribution of wealth is relatively balanced, although social inequalities have risen in recent years. The Finnish system fits into the Nordic conception of social welfare, except benefits are lower in some categories, such as sickness and unemployment payments. The social welfare system in Finland embraces the model adopted by the Nordic nations, generally featuring: high taxes a large public sector, broad universal services and support, productive investment in health, education, and job training and strong work incentives.[73]

Finland has a multi-party system which ensures that a single party does not have a chance to gain power alone.[74] Parties work with each other to form coalition governments. The Finns Party is a far-right, anti-Muslim political party. Founded in 1995, it has become one of the country's largest political parties. The Finns were part of a 2015 government coalition and became the second largest party in the 2015 and 2019 national elections.

Since its founding, the party has embraced the nativist identity politics of Finnish nationalism. Anti-immigration rhetoric is one of the signature themes of the party. It combines left-wing economic policies with conservative social values, socio-cultural authoritarianism, and ethnic nationalism. The party's current profile has been compared to other European far-right parties such as the Sweden Democrats and France's National Rally.[75]

The Finns Party is currently the second largest party represented in the Finnish parliament. Established in 1995, it is the successor to the Finnish Rural Party, which was disbanded in the early 1990's. Its platform and policies are built on work ethic, entrepreneurship, and a balanced social welfare system linked to Christian values. The party's members are cautious about corporatism, support the free market economy, and believe in the distribution of wealth to help disadvantaged citizens. Furthermore, they contend that the EU membership costs are too high and that Finland should re-evaluate and negotiate its current membership.[76]

In the past decade, populist parties have gained support in European politics, disrupting the old regime of left-right parties.[77] Although populist parties have existed for many years, the financial crisis of the late 2000s and the surge in the number of refugees from impoverished and war-torn countries have contributed to the rise of populism in recent years. Populist parties often utilize the discourse of "othering," blaming out-groups for crises and framing them as potential threats to the nation. Any crisis or disruption of the status quo is a potential opportunity for seeking a scapegoat, as well as questioning the existing system of governance. This appeals to many voters who are concerned about economic and cultural changes.[78]

The main concerns of the Finns Party concerns are public finances, the defense and security of the homeland, care for Finns and being Finnish, competitiveness and priority for entrepreneurs, and stopping bullying. The first concern is related to bridging solutions to the sustainability gap in the public sector, which, in their opinion, can be accomplished by cutting support for immigration and foreign aid, managing and restricting indebtedness, reasonable taxation, a tax-free income of 1000 € month, and removing taxes on passenger vehicles. The second security-related concern arose largely due to the financial crisis, and the solutions include budget increases and careful consideration of joining NATO. The third concern is about the growing number of Finns living on or under the poverty line, which requires an evaluation of the social security system.

The private sector is seen as the foundation of general welfare; to maintain it, current energy and climate policies must be changed, and the green tax decreased. According to the Finns, part of the solution is to terminate the EU's bureaucracy and recognizing a child's right to a mother and a father. In the past decade, the party has attracted increasing numbers of voters due to its ethnic nationalistic approach to immigration, conservative social values, and left-wing economic policies.[79] Some Finns Party MP's and other elected officials have been criticized for their racist remarks on various platforms. Political scandals relating to unacceptable talk or behavior have increased within the Finns Party.[80]

British National Party

As a former colonial power, England has long had an ethnic minority population. Many of them were from former British colonies. Anti-immigrant sentiment began to emerge not long after the arrival of significant numbers of ethnic minorities after the Second World War. Enoch Powell was an influential Member of Parliament who vigorously advocated against immigrants. In his infamous 1968 "Rivers of Blood" speech delivered in Birmingham, England, Powell said, "[a]s I look ahead, I am filled with forbidding. Like the Roman, I seem to see 'the River Tiber foaming with much blood'. That tragic and intractable phenomenon which we watch with horror on the other side of the Atlantic . . . is coming upon us here by our own volition and our own neglect.[81] Powell invoked an image of England overrun by non-white immigrants.[82]

The "phenomenon" to which he alluded was race riots that erupted in several American cities during the late 1960s. The speech resonated with many white, working-class Britons who regarded Powell as a true patriot. In a 1978 speech, Margaret Thatcher, who served as Prime Minister of the United Kingdom from 1979 to 1990, expressed similar sentiments. She blamed ethnic minority immigrants for the rising crime rate, street violence, and misuse of welfare benefits. Commenting on the growing number of ethnic minority immigrants, Thatcher said:

> I think it means that people are really rather afraid that this country might be rather swamped by people with a different culture. The British character has done so much for democracy, for law, and done so much throughout the world, that if there is any fear that it might be swamped, people are going to react and be rather hostile to those coming in. . . . We are a British nation with British characteristics. Every nation can take some minorities, and in many ways, they add to the richness and variety of this country. But the moment a minority threatens to become a big one, people get frightened.[83]

The British National Party (BNP) is a far-right political party that strongly opposes the immigration of non-whites. The party "stands for the preservation of the national and ethnic character of the British people and is wholly opposed to any form of racial integration between British and non-European peoples." It is "committed to stemming and reversing the tide of non-white immigration and to restoring, by legal changes, negotiation, and consent, the overwhelmingly white makeup of the British population that existed in Britain prior to 1948." The BNP advocates the use of "firm but voluntary incentives" to remove ethnic minorities from Britain. BNP membership is restricted to "Indigenous Caucasian[s]."[84]

Conclusion

The migration crisis in Europe has been a significant and ongoing issue, with various factors contributing to the influx of migrants and refugees. In recent years, hundreds of thousands of people have made dangerous journeys to Europe, fleeing war, poverty, and natural disasters. The crisis has also had significant political consequences, fueling support for far-right political parties and increasing political polarization across Europe. Wars and conflicts in countries like Syria, Afghanistan, and parts of Africa force people to seek asylum elsewhere.

Poverty and lack of economic opportunities in many regions, particularly in sub-Saharan Africa, drive people to migrate in search of better livelihoods. Natural disasters and climate change, such as droughts and floods, displace communities and force them to move. This anti-immigration sentiment in Europe arises from the perception of immigrants as a threat. First, the belief that immigrants lower wages and limit job options for native workers constitutes the economic threat of the immigrants. In addition, the burden that immigrants bring to the welfare system is used to paint immigrants as a financial burden to the country. But while the perceived financial and economic threats of immigrants are significant, the main driver of the anti-immigration movement in Europe is the symbolic threat that immigrants present to the national culture and values.

Notes

1 Hans Kohn, Encyclopedia Britannica, *Nationalism*, https://www.britannica.com/topic/nationalism (last updated Feb. 19, 2020).

2 Cass Muddle and Cristobal Rovira Kaltwasser, *The Far Right Today, Populism: A Very Short Introduction* (Oxford University Press, 2017).

3 Jean Renaud Gabriel Camus and Nellie Bowles, *You Will Not Replace Us!* (self-published, 2012); Nellie Bowles, Replacement Theory, a Racist, Sexist Doctrine, Spreads in Far-Right Circles, *New York Times*, https://www.nytimes.com/2019/03/18/technology/replacement-theory.html (last updated Mar. 18, 2019).

4 Camus and Bowles.

5 Omer Karasapan, Refugees, Migrants, and the Politics of Fear, *Brookings*, https://www.brookings.edu/blog/future-development/2017/04/12/refugees-migrants-and-the-politics-of-fear/ (last updated Apr. 12, 2017).

6 Christchurch Mosque Attack: Brenton Tarrant Sentenced to Life Without Parole, *BBC*, https://www.bbc.com/news/world-asia-53919624 (last updated Aug. 27, 2020).

7 Tim Arango, Nicholas Bogel-Burroughs and Katie Benner, Minutes Before El Paso Killing, Hate-Filled Manifesto Appears Online, *New York Times*, https://www.nytimes.com/2019/08/03/us/patrick-crusius-el-paso-shooter-manifesto.html (last updated Aug. 3, 2019); Rosa Schwartzburg, The 'White Replacement Theory' Motivates Alt-Right Killers the World over, *The Guardian*, https://www.theguardian.com/commentisfree/2019/aug/05/great-replacement-theory-alt-right-killers-el-paso (last updated Aug. 5, 2019).

8 Hawes Spencer and Sheryl Gay Stolberg, White Nationalists March on University of Virginia New York Times, *The New York Times*, https://www.nytimes.com/2017/08/11/us/white-nationalists-rally-charlottesville-virginia.html (last updated Aug. 11, 2017).

9 Economic and Social Survey 2017, *Post-War Reconstruction and Development in the Golden Age of Capitalism* (2017), https://www.un.org/development/desa/dpad/wp-content/uploads/sites/45/WESS_2017_ch2.pdf.

10 See generally, Tjitske Akkerman, Sarah de Lange and Matthijs Rooduijn, *Right-Wing Populist Parties in Western Europe* (Manuela Caiani and Ondřej Císař, eds., Routledge, 2016).

11 Akkerman, de Lange and Rooduijn.

12 Akkerman, de Lange and Rooduijn.

13 Evan Burr Bukey, *Hitler's Austria: Popular Sentiment in the Nazi Era, 1938–1945* (University of North Carolina Press, 2000).

14 Austria's Far-Right Freedom Party Sets Up Panel to Examine Its Past, *Reuters*, https://www.reuters.com/article/us-austria-politics-freedom-party/austrias-far-right-freedom-party-sets-up-panel-to-examine-its-past-idUSKCN1FX1PN (last updated Feb. 13, 2018).

15 Farid Hafez, Reinhard Heinisch and Eric Miklin, The New Right Austria's Freedom Party and Changing Perceptions of Islam, *Brookings*, https://www.brookings.edu/research/the-new-right-austrias-freedom-party-and-changing-perceptions-of-islam (last updated Jul. 24, 2019); Lothar Höbelt, *Defiant Populist: Jörg Haider and the Politics of Austria* (Purdue University Press, 2000)

16 Ruth Wodak, *The Politics of Fear: What Right-Wing Populist Discourses Mean* (SAGE Publications Ltd, 2015).

17 Paul Hockenos, *Jörg Haider: Austria's Far Right Wunderkind*, 12(3) World Pol'y J. 75–80 (1995); Lothar Höbelt, *Defiant Populist: Jörg Haider and the Politics of Austria* (Purdue University Press, 2000).

18 Reuters, Views Under Fire; Words That Ignited a Diplomatic Crisis, *The New York Times*, https://www.nytimes.com/2000/02/01/world/views-under-fire-words-that-ignited-a-diplomatic-crisis.html (last updated Feb. 1, 2000).

19 Anton Pelinka, *The Haider Phenomenon in Austria: Examining the FPO in European Context, Fall 2001*, 9(1) J. Int'l Inst. (2009), https://quod.lib.umich.edu/j/jii/4750978.0009.102/--haider-phenomenon-in-austria-examining-the-fpo-in-european?rgn=main;view=fulltext.

20 Austria Passes Controversial Reforms to 1912 Islam Law, *BBC News*, https://www.bbc.com/news/world-europe-31629543 (last updated Feb. 25, 2015).

21 Austrian Ban on Full-Face Veil in Public Places Comes into Force, *BBC News*, https://www.bbc.com/news/world-europe-41457427 (last updated Oct. 1, 2017).

22 Nicholas Kulish and Eugen Freund, Jörg Haider, Austrian Rightist, Is Dead at 58, *The New York Times*, https://www.nytimes.com/2008/10/12/world/europe/12iht-12haider.16875210.html (last updated Oct. 12, 2000).

23 Austria's Far-Right Freedom Party Ministers All Resign Amid Scanda, *BBC News*, https://www.bbc.com/news/world-europe-48335316?intlink_from_url=&link_location=live-reporting-story (last updated May 20, 2019).

24 History of the Flemish Federated Entity and Its Parliamentary Assemblies, *Flemish Parliament*, https://www.flemishparliament.eu/about-the-flemish-parliament/history-the-flemish-federated-entity-and-its-parliamentary-assemblies.

25 Beaufays, Jean, *"Belgium: A Dualist Political System?" Publius* 18(2) JSTOR, 63–73 (1988), http://www.jstor.org/stable/3330461 (last visited Dec. 25, 2019).

26 Ian Traynor, The Language Divide at the Heart of a Split That Is Tearing Belgium Apart, *The Guardian*, https://www.theguardian.com/world/2010/may/09/belgium-flanders-wallonia-french-dutch (last updated May 8, 2010).

27 Higgins, A Close Look at Brussels Offers a More Nuanced View of Radicalization, *New York Times*, https://www.nytimes.com/2016/04/20/world/europe/more-than-islam-origin-is-a-marker-for-terror-among-brussels-immigrants.html (last updated Apr. 19, 2016); Freddy Merkx and Liz Fekete, Belgium: The Racist Cocktail, *Race and Class*, https://journals.sagepub.com/doi/abs/10.1177/030639689103200307?journalCode=racb (last updated Jan. 1, 1991).

28 Eva Brems, *Belgium: The Vlaams Blok Political Party Convicted Indirectly of Racism*, 4(4) Int'l J. Const. L. 702–11 (2006), https://doi.org/10.1093/icon/mol032.

29 Laurens Cerulo, Inside the Far Right's Flemish Victory, *Politico*, https://www.politico.eu/article/inside-the-far-rights-flemish-victory/ (last updated May 27, 2019).

30 Tjitske Akkerman, The Impact of Populist Radical-Right Parties on Immigration Policy Agendas: A Look at the Netherlands, *Migration Policy Institute*, https://www.migrationpolicy.org/research/populist-radical-right-parties-immigration-netherlands (last updated Jul. 2008).

31 Tom-Jan Meeus, The Wilders Effect: How the Far-Right Rabble-Rouser Hijacked Dutch Politics, *Politico*, https://www.politico.eu/article/the-geert-wilders-effect-dutch-politics-mark-rutte-elections/ (last updated Feb. 8, 2007).

32 Europe's Growing Muslim Population, *Pew Research Center*, https://www.pewforum.org/2017/11/29/europes-growing-muslim-population (last updated Nov. 29, 2017).

33 Provocateurs Death Haunts the Dutch, *New York Times*, https://www.nytimes.com/2014/11/02/arts/provocateurs-death-haunts-the-dutch-.html (last updated Nov. 14, 2014).

34 Frank Kool, Remembering Pim Fortuyn, *Dutch Review*, https://dutchreview.com/culture/history/remembering-pim-fortuyn/ (last updated May 6, 2018).

35 Koen Damhuis, "The Biggest Problem in the Netherlands": Understanding the Party for Freedom's Politicization of Islam, *Brookings*, https://www.brookings.edu/research/the-biggest-problem-in-the-netherlands-understanding-the-party-for-freedoms-politicization-of-islam (last updated Jul. 24, 2019).

36 Geert Wilders, *Marked for Death: Islam's War Against the West and Me* (Regnery Publishing, 2012).

37 Ban the Koran in the Netherlands, Says Far-Right Leader Wilders, *Euronews*, https://www.euronews.com/2017/03/05/ban-the-koran-in-the-netherlands-says-far-right-leader-wilders (last updated May 3, 2017).

38 Billy Ehrenberg-Shannon and Aleksandra Wisniewska, How Education Level Is the Biggest Predictor of Support for Geert Wilders, *Financial Times*, https://www.ft.com/dutchvoting (last updated Mar. 2, 2017); Catherine E. de Vries and Isabell Hoffmann, Who Does Support Geert Wild, *Eupinions Brief*, https://eupinions.eu/de/text/who-does-support-geert-wilders (last updated Mar. 14, 2017).

39 https://www.britannica.com/topic/Northern-League.

40 Catherine Edwards, Political Cheat Sheet: Understanding Italy's Northern League, *The Local*, https://www.thelocal.it/20180118/political-cheat-sheet-understanding-italys-northern-league (last updated Jan. 18, 2018).

41 Catherine Edwards, Political Cheat Sheet: Understanding Italy's Northern League, *The Local*, https://www.thelocal.it/20180118/political-cheat-sheet-understanding-italys-northern-league (last updated Jan. 18, 2018).

42 UNHCR, https://www.unhcr.org/en-us/europe.html.

43 Migration and Home Affairs, *European Commision*, https://ec.europa.eu/home-affairs/what-we-do/policies/asylum_en.

44 Eugenio Cusumano and Kristof Gombeer, *In Deep Waters: The Legal, Humanitarian and Political Implications of Closing Italian Ports to Migrant Rescuers*, 25(2) Mediterranean Pol. 245–53 (2020), doi: 10.1080/13629395.2018.1532145.

45 Lorenzo Tonda, Matteo Salvini Goes on Trial over Migrant Kidnapping Charges, *The Guardian*, https://www.theguardian.com/world/2020/oct/02/matteo-salvini-set-to-be-tried-over-migrant-kidnapping-charges-italy (last updated Oct. 2, 2020).

46 Italy's Salvini to Face New Trial over Migrant Ship Blockade, *BBC News*, https://www.bbc.com/news/world-europe-53592852 (last updated Jul. 30, 2020).

47 Jason Horowitz, New Government Takes Shape in Italy, Sidelining Salvini and the Hard-Right, *New York Times*, https://www.nytimes.com/2019/08/28/world/europe/italy-government-salvini.html (last updated Aug. 28, 2019).

48 Johan Bjerkem, The Norwegian Progress Party: An Established Populist Party, *European View*, 15, 233–43, https://doi.org/10.1007/s12290-016-0404–8 (last updated Dec. 1, 2016).

49 Information in English, *Fremskrittspartiet*, https://www.frp.no/english.

50 Johan Bjerkem, The Norwegian Progress Party: An Established Populist Party, *European View*, 15, https://doi.org/10.1007/s12290-016-0404–8 (last updated Dec. 1, 2016).

51 The Nordic Model May Be the Best Cushion Against Capitalism. Can It Survive Immigration? *New York Times*, https://www.nytimes.com/2019/07/11/business/sweden-economy-immigration.html (last updated Jul. 11, 2019).

52 Johan Bjerkem, The Norwegian Progress Party: An Established Populist Party, *European View*, 15, 233–43, https://doi.org/10.1007/s12290-016-0404–8 (last updated Dec. 1, 2016).

53 Norway Party Quits Government in 'Jihadist-Wife' Row, *BBC News*, https://www.bbc.com/news/world-europe-51174550 (last updated Jan. 20, 2020)

54 Kirsti M. Jylhä, Jens Rydgren and Pontus Strimling, *Radical Right-Wing Voters from Right and Left: Comparing Sweden Democrat Voters Who Previously Voted for the Conservative Party or the Social Democratic Party*, 42(3–4) Scandinavian Pol. Stud. (2019), https://onlinelibrary.wiley.com/doi/pdf/10.1111/1467-9477.12147.

55 *The Swedish Model*, https://www.government.se/4a5336/contentassets/8416c4ff1410419090181fe503920390/the-swedish-model.pd.

56 Danielle Lee Thomson, The Rise of Sweden Democrats: Islam, Populism and the End of Swedish Exceptionalism, *Brookings*, https://www.brookings.edu/research/the-rise-of-sweden-democrats-and-the-end-of-swedish-exceptionalism/ (last updated Mar. 25, 2020).

57 G. Erlingsson, K. Vernby, and R. Öhrvall, *The Single-Issue Party Thesis and the Sweden Democrats*, 49 Acta Polit 196–216 (2014), https://doi.org/10.1057/ap.2013.18; G. Elgenius and J. Rydgren, *Democrats and the Ethno-Nationalist Rhetoric of Decay and Betrayal*, 38 Swed. (2017).

58 G. Elgenius and J. Rydgren, The Sweden Democrats and the Ethno-Nationalist Rhetoric of Decay and Betrayal, *Diva*, 2017, https://www.diva-portal.org/smash/record.jsf?pid=diva2%3A1168350&dswid=6244; D. Mulinari and A. Neergaard, *The Sweden Democrats, Racisms and the Construction of the Muslim Threat. Global Islamophobia: Muslims and Moral Panic in the West*, 67–82 (2012).

59 Migrant Crisis: Migration to Europe Explained in Seven Charts, *BBC News*, https://www.bbc.com/news/world-europe-34131911 (last updated Mar. 4, 2016).

60 Heba Habib, Outrage After Far-Right Swedish MP Goes to Greece and Gives Refugees Leaflets Saying: "We're Full—Don't Come!," *Independent*, https://www.independent.co.uk/news/world/europe/sweden-full-leaflets-greece-refugees-jimmie-akesson-a9383996.html (last updated Mar. 6, 2020); https://www.google.com/maps/place/Edirne,+Edirne+Merkez%2FEdirne,+Turkey/@41.6689063,26.5558148,14z/data=!3m1!4b1!4m5!3m4!1s0x14b32f77a26304e1:0xa0cfc0ca431c30bc!8m2!3d41.6771297!4d26.5557145.

61 Populist Sweden Democrats Ditch 'Swexit' Ahead of EU Elections, *Reuters*, https://www.reuters.com/article/uk-sweden-politics-eu/populist-sweden-democrats-ditch-swexit-ahead-of-eu-elections-idUKKCN1PV28.

62 Jacob Torfing, *Local Forms of Governance in Denmark: The Revenge of the Supplement*, 3(3) J. Power 405–25 (2010), doi: 10.1080/17540291.2010.524993.

63 Susi Meret, Islam and the Danish-Scandinavian Welfare State, A 'Muslims in the West' Reaction Essay, *Brookings*, https://www.brookings.edu/articles/

islam-and-the-danish-scandinavian-welfare-state/ (last updated Dec. 4, 2019); Danish Muslims Feel Backlash as Immigration Becomes Election Issue, *Dansk Folkparti*, https://danskfolkeparti.dk/politik/in-another-languages-politics/1757-2/%20Stine%20Jacobson (last updated May 31, 2019); https://www.reuters.com/article/us-denmark-election-immigration/danish-muslims-feel-backlash-.

64 Denmark Election: Anti-EU Danish People's Party Gets Big Boost, *BBC News*, https://www.bbc.com/news/world-europe-33199488 (last updated Jun. 19, 2015).

65 The Issue of Depicting the Prophet Muhammad, *BBC News*, https://www.bbc.com/news/world-europe-30813742 (last updated Jan. 14, 2015).

66 Laura Smith-Spark, Denmark's Parliament Bans Wearing of Face Veils in Public, *CNN*, https://www.cnn.com/2018/05/31/europe/denmark-face-veil-ban-intl/index.html (last updated May 31, 2018).

67 Niels Finn Christiansen and Klaus Petersen, *The Dynamics of Social Solidarity: The Danish Welfare State, 1900–2000*, 26(3) Scandinavian J. Hist. 177–96 (2001).

68 Christoffer Green- Pedersen and Jesper Krogstrup, *Immigration as a Political Issue in Denmark and Sweden*, 47 Eur. J. Pol. Res. 610–34 (2008), doi:10.1111/j.1475-6765.2008. 00777.x.

69 In Denmark, Harsh New Laws for Immigrant "Ghettos," *New York Times*, https://www.nytimes.com/2018/07/01/world/europe/denmark-immigrant-ghettos.html (last updated Jul. 1, 2018).

70 Lisa Abend-Vornberg, An Island for "Unwanted" Migrants Is Denmark's Latest Aggressive Anti-Immigrant Policy, *Time*, https://time.com/5504331/denmark-migrants-lindholm-island/ (last updated Jan. 16, 2019).

71 Anders Ravik Juskas, Why Did the Danish People's Party Lose More Than Fifty Percent of Its Votes? *Uio,c-REX- Center for Research on Extremism*, https://www.sv.uio.no/c-rex/english/news-and-events/right-now/2019/danish-election-2019.html (last updated Jun. 6, 2019).

72 Seppo Zetterberg, MAIN OUTLINES OF FINNISH HISTORY Swedish, Russian and Independent Eras in a Nutshel, *This Is Finland*, https://finland.fi/life-society/main-outlines-of-finnish-history/ (last updated May 2017).

73 Social Welfare in Finland, *Brochures of the Ministry of Social Affairs and Health*, 2006, https://julkaisut.valtioneuvosto.fi/bitstream/handle/10024/70241/Es200611eng.pdf?sequence=1.

74 Jarmo Laine, Parliamentarism in Finland, *This Is Finland*, https://finland.fi/life-society/parliamentarism-in-finland/ (last modified Jun. 2019).

75 Finns Party—in English, *Peruss*, https://www.perussuomalaiset.fi/kielisivu/in-english/.

76 M. K. Criss, *Language, Immigration, and Identity: An Analysis of the Discourses of the Finns Party*, 19(2) J. Language & Pol. 270–89 (2020), doi: 10.1075/jlp.19044.cri.

77 Jan Sundberg, Who Are the Nationalist Finns Party? *BBC*, https://www.bbc.com/news/world-europe-32627013 (last updated May 11, 2015).

78 Inari Sakki and Katarina Pettersson, *Discursive Constructions of Otherness in Populist Radical Right Political Blogs*, Eur. J. Soc. Psychol. 156–70 (2016).

79 Ainur Elgren, The Nordic Ideal: Openness and Populism According to the Finns Party in the Paradox of Opennessn, *Brill*, https://brill.com/view/book/edcoll/9789004281196/B9789004281196-s007.xm.

80 *The European Mainstream and the Populist Radical Right* (Pontus Odmalm and Eve Hepburn, eds., Routledge, 2017); Finnish MP Loses Committee Post After Racist Remarks, *Reuters*, https://www.reuters.com/article/uk-finland-finns/finnish-mp-loses-committee-post-after-racist-remarks-idUKBRE85C0ST20120613 (last updated Jun. 13, 2012); Finns Party Leader Halla-Aho Says He Condemns Racial Prejudice, *Uutiset*, https://yle.fi/uutiset/osasto/news/finns_party_leader_halla-aho_says_he_condemns_racial_prejudice/11624733 (last updated Oct. 31, 2020).

81 The Telegraph, https://www.telegraph.co.uk/news/0/enoch-powells-rivers-blood-speech/ (last updated Nov. 6, 2007).

82 Samuel Earle, Rivers of Blood: The Legacy of a Speech That Divided Britain, *The Atlantic*, https://www.theatlantic.com/international/archive/2018/04/enoch-powell-rivers-of-blood/558344/ (last updated Apr. 20, 2018).

83 TV Interview for Granada World in Action ("Rather Swamped"), *Margret Thatcher Foundation*, https://www.margaretthatcher.org/document/10348.

84 STOPPING ALL IMMIGRATION: At the Core of British National Party Policy Is the Belief That Immigration Into Britain Is a Destructive Agenda and Must Be Stopped, *BNP*, https://bnp.org.uk/policies/immigration/.

Bibliography

Aboud, Frances E. and Amato, Maria, *Developmental and Socialization Influence on Intergroup Bias*, in Blackwell Handbook of Social Psychology: Intergroup Processes, 65–89 (Rupert Brown and Samuel Gaertner, eds., Blackwell Publishing, 2003).

Akkerman, Tjitske, de Lange, Sarah and Rooduijn, Matthijs, *Right-Wing Populist Parties in Western Europe* (Manuela Caiani and Ondřej Císař, eds., Routledge, 2016).

Alloula, Malek, *The Colonial Harem* (University of Minnesota Press, 1986).

Anderson, Elijah, The Code of the Streets, *The Atlantic Monthly,* May 1994, http://www.theatlantic.com/magazine/archive/1994/05/the-code-of-the-streets/306601.

Anderson, James D., *Education of Blacks in the South 1860–1835* (1988). The African American education Databook volume II preschool through high school education.

Anderson, Martin, *The Federal Bulldozer: A Critical Analysis of Urban Renewal, 1949-1962* (M.I.T. Press, 1964).

Arango, Tim, Bogel-Burroughs, Nicholas and Benner, Katie, Minutes Before El Paso Killing, -Filled Manifesto Appears Online, *New York Times*, https://www.nytimes.com/2019/08/03/us/patrick-crusius-el-paso-shooter-manifesto.html.

Armour, Jody, *Stereotypes and Prejudice: Helping Legal Decisionmakers Break the Prejudice Habit*, 83 Calif. L. Rev. 733, 741–55 (1995).

Atiba, Phillip et al., *The Essence of Innocence: Consequences of Dehumanizing Black*, 106 Children J. Pers. Soc. Psych. 526, 531 (2014).

Benbow, Mark E., *Birth of a Quotation: Woodrow Wilson and "Like Writing History with Lightning*, 9(4) JGAPE 509-33 (2010), http://www.jstor.org/stable/20799409.

Berman v. Parker, 348 U.S 26. (1954).

Blake, Jamilia J. et al., *Unmasking the Inequitable Discipline Experiences of Urban Black Girls: Implications for Urban Educational Stakeholders*, 43(1) Urban Rev. 90–106 (2010).

Board of Education of Oklahoma City v. Dowell, 498 US 237 (1991).

Bobo, Lawrence, *Racial Attitudes and Relations at the Close of the Twentieth Century*, in America Becoming: Racial Trends and Their Consequences, 264, 273–80 (Neil J. Smelser, William Julius Wilson, and Faith Mitchell, eds., National Academy Press, 2001).

Bobo, Lawrence and Kluegel, James, *Status, Idealogy and Dimensions of White's Racial Beliefs and Attitudes: Progress and Stagnation*, in Racial Attitudes in the 1990s

Continuity and Change, 99–105 (Steven A. Tuch and Jack K. Martin, eds., Praeger, 1997).
Bogle, Donald, *Toms, Coons, Mulattoes, Mammies, and Bucks: An Interpretive History of Blacks in American Films* (Bloomsbury Academic, 1989).
Bogle, Donald, *Primetime Blues: African Americans on Network Television*, 26–42 (Farrar, Straus, and Giroux, 2001).
Bowles, Nellie, Replacement Theory, a Racist, Sexist Doctrine, Spreads in Far-Right Circles, *New York Times*, https://www.nytimes.com/2019/03/18/technology/replacement-theory.htm.
Britannica, T., Editors of Encyclopedia. "Atlanta Compromise," *Encyclopedia Britannica*, Jul. 27, 2020. https://www.britannica.com/event/Atlanta-Compromise.
Brown v. Board of Education of Topeka, 349 US 294 (1955).
Buchanan v. Warley, 245 US 60 (1917).
Bukey, Evan Burr, *Hitler's Austria: Popular Sentiment in the Nazi Era, 1938–1945* (University of North Carolina Press, 2000).
Camus, Jean Renaud Gabriel, *Categorization*, in Studies in Cross Cultural Psychology 1, 1–2 (Neil Warren ed., 1977).
Camus, Jean Renaud Gabriel, *You Will Not Replace Us!* (self-published, 2012).
Caro, Robert A., *The Power Broker: Robert Moses and the Fall of New York* (Knopf, 1975).
Carroll, Charles, *"The Negro a Beast" or "In the Image of God"* (Lushena Books, 1900).
Carter, Prudence, et al., *You Can't Fix What You Don't Look At: Acknowledging Race In Addressing Racial Discipline Disparities* (The Atlantic Philanthropies, 2014).
Carter, Robert L., *A Matter of Law: A Memoir* (New Press, 2005).
Christchurch Mosque Attack: Brenton Tarrant Sentenced to Life Without Parole, *BBC*, https://www.bbc.com/news/world-asia-53919624.
Civil Rights Cases 109 US 3 (1883).
Civil Rights Data Collection, U.S. Dep't of Educ. Office for Civil rights, issue brief no. 1, 1 Data Snapshot (School Discipline) 24 (2014), http://ocrdata.ed.gov/downloads/crdc-school-discipline-snapshot.pdf.
Cottrol, Robert J., Diamond, Raymond T., and Ware, Leland, *Brown v. Board of Education: Caste, Culture and the Constitution* (University Press of Kansas, 2003)
Davis, Michael and Clark, Hunter R., *Thurgood Marshall: Warrior at the Bar, Rebel on the Bench* (Carol Publishing Corporation, 1992).
Davis, Peggy C., *Law as Microaggression*, 98 Yale L. J. 1559, 1561–2 (1989).
de Lange, Sarah and Rooduijn, Matthijs, *Right-Wing Populist Parties in Western Europe* (Manuela Caiani and Ondřej Císař, eds., Routledge, 2016).

Dikec, Mustafa, *Badlands of the Republic: Space, Politics and Urban Policy* (Wiley, 2007).

DiMento, Joseph F. C. and Ellis, Cliff, *Changing Lanes:Visions and Histories of Urban Freeways* (The MIT Press, 2013).

Dixon, Thomas, *The Clansman: An Historical Romance of the Ku Klux* (Press of Braunworth & Co., 1905).

Du Bois, W. E. B, Letter to NAACP Board of Directors, Jun. 26, 1934, https://credo.library.umass.edu/view/full/mums312-b071-i296.

Duroy, Quentin, *North African Identity and Racial Discrimination in France: A Social Economic Analysis of Capability Deprivation*, Rev. Soc. Econ., 307 315–16 (2011).

Earle, Samuel, Rivers of Blood, *The Atlantic*, https://www.theatlantic.com/international/archive/2018/04/enoch-powell-rivers-of-blood/558344/.

Economic and Social Survey 2017, *Post-War Reconstruction and Development in the Golden Age of Capitalism* (2017), https://www.un.org/development/desa/dpad/wp-content/uploads/sites/45/WESS_2017_ch2.pdf.

Ewen, Elizabeth and Ewen, Stuart, *Typecasting: On the Arts & Sciences of Human Inequality*, 407–13 (Seven Stories Press, 2006).

Ezorsky, Gertrude, *Racism and Justice: The Case for Affirmative Action*, 62 (Cornell University Press, 1991).

Fanon, Frantz, *A Dying Colonialism* (Grove Press, 1965).

Ferry, Jules François Camille, Speech Before the French Chamber of Deputies, Mar. 28, 1 884, *Modern History Sourcebook: Jules Ferry (1832–1893): On French Colonial Expansion*, http://www.fordham.edu/halsall/mod/1884ferry.asp.

Fishman, Robert, *Urban Utopias in the Twentieth Century: Ebenezer Howard, Frank Lloyd Wright, Le Corbusier* (Basic Books Inc., ; 1st ed., 1977).

Foner, Eric, *Reconstruction: America's Unfinished Revolution, 1863–1877* (Perennial Classics, 1988).

Fox, Kenneth, *Metropolitan America, Urban Life and Urban Policy in the United States, 1940–1980* (University Press of Mississippi, 1990).

Foxx, Anthony, More Than Engineering: Infrastructure Shapes Places, *Urban Institute*, Jan. 16, 2018, https://www.urban.org/infrastructure/more-engineering-infrastructure-shapes-places.

Freeman v. Pitts, 498 US 1081 (1992).

Freund, David M. P., *Colored Property: State Policy and White Racial Politics in Suburban America* (The University of Chicago Press, 2010).

Gaertner, Samuel L. and Dovidio, John F., The Aversive Form of Racism, in *Prejudice, Discrimination and Racism: Theory and Research*, 61–89 (John F. Dovidio and Samuel L. Gaertner, eds., Academic Press, 1986).

Gaertner, Samuel L. and Dovidio, John F., *Reducing Intergroup Bias: The Common Ingroup Identity Model*, 24–6 (Routledge, 2000).

Gans, Herbert J., Symbolic Ethnicity: The Future of Ethnic Groups and Cultures in America, 2(1), 1–20 (1979), DOI: 10.1080/01419870.1979.9993248.

George, Joel, *Stereotype and School Pushout: Race, Gender, and Discipline Disparities*, 68 Ark. L. Rev. 101, 107–9 (2015).

Gershenson, Seth, Stephen B. Holt, and Nicholas W. Papageorge. Who Believes in Me?: *The Effect of Student-Teacher Demographic Match on Teacher Expectations*. Upjohn Institute Working Paper 15–231.W.E. Upjohn Institute for Employment Research, 2015). https://doi.org/10.17848/ wp15–231.

Gordon, Adam, *The Creation of Homeownership: How New Deal Changes in Banking Regulation Simultaneously Made Homeownership Accessible to Whites and Out of Reach for Blacks*, 186 Yale L. J. 115, 207 (2005).

Gotham, Kevin Fox, *A City without Slums: Urban Renewal, Public Housing, and Downtown Revitalization in Kansas City, Missouri*, 60(1) Am. J. Econ. Sociol., Special Issue: City and Country: An Interdisciplinary Collection: 285–316 (2001).

Green v. County Sch. Bd. of New Kent County, 391 US 430 (1968).

Greenberg, Jack, *Crusaders in the Courts: How a Dedicated Band of Lawyers Fought for the Civil Rights Revolution* (Basic Books, 1994).

Greenberg, Stanley B., *Middle Class Dreams: The Politics and Power of the New American Majority*, 23–54 (Yale University Press, 1995, rev. ed. 1996).

Greenwald, Anthony G. T., Andrew, Poehlman, Uhlmann, Eric Luis and Banaji, Mahzarin R., *Understanding and Using the Implicit Association Test: III. Meta-Analysis of Predictive Validity*, 97 J. Persp. Soc. Psychol. 17–41 (2009).

Griffin v. School Board, 375 US 391 (1964).

Hafez, Farid, Heinisch, Reinhard and Miklin, Eric, The New Right Austria's Freedom Party and Changing Perceptions of Islam, *Brookings*, https://www.brookings.edu/research/the-new-right-austrias-freedom-party-and-changing-perceptions-of-islam.

Hainsworth, Paul, *The Extreme Right in France: The Rise and Rise of Jean-Marie Le Pen's Front National*, 40(2) Representation 101–14 (2004).

Hale, Dana S., *French Images of Race on Product Trademarks During the Third Republic, in, The Color of Liberty, Histories of Race in France* (Duke University Press, 2003).

Harlan, Louis R., *Booker T. Washington: The Making of a Black Leader, 1856–1901* (Oxford University Press, Feb. 13, 1975).

Harris, Joel Chandler, *Uncle Remus; Tales* (Beehive Press, 1974).

Hawes, Spencer and Sheryl, Gay Stolberg, White Nationalists March on University of Virginia New York Times, *The New York Times*, https://www.nytimes.com/2017/08/11/us/white-nationalists-rally-charlottesville-.

Hinojosa, Melanie S. and Mora, Amanda, *Challenging Colorblind Education: A Descriptive Analysis of Teacher Racial Attitudes*, 4(2) Soc. Faculty Publications 28–30 (2009), http://digitalcommons.sacredheart.edu/cgi/viewcontent.cgi?article=1005&context=sociol_fac

Historically, Voters Don't Follow the Front National's Advice, *LeFigaro*, Apr. 26, 2012, http://plus.lefigaro.fr/note/historically-voters-dont-follow-the-front-nationals-advice-20120426-905492,

Höbelt, Lothar, *Defiant Populist: Jörg Haider and the Politics of Austria* (Purdue University Press, 2000).

Hockenos, Paul, *Jörg Haider: Austria's Far Right Wunderkind*, 12(3) World Pol'y J. 75–80 (1995).

Hosford, Desmond and Wojtkowski, Chong J. (eds.), *French Orientalism: Culture, Politics and the Imagined Other* (Cambridge Scholars Publishing, 2010).

Howell, Benjamin, *Exploiting Race and Space: Concentrated Subprime Lending as Housing Discrimination,* 94 Calif. L. Rev 101, 112 (2006).

Hoyt, Homer, *The Structure and Growth of Residential Neighborhoods in American Cities* (Federal Housing Administration, 1939).

Hoyt, Homer, *One Hundred Years of Land Values in Chicago* (public domain, 1933).

Hurwitz, Jon, and Peffley, Mark, eds., *Perception and Prejudice: Race and Politics in the United States* (Yale University Press, 1998).

Irons, Peter H., *Jim Crow's Children: The Broken Promise of the Brown Decision* (Penguin Books, 2002).

Jackson, John L., *Racial Paranoia: The Unintended Consequences of Political Correctness,* 81–110 (Basic Civitas Books, 2008).

Jackson, Kenneth T., *Crabgrass Frontier: The Suburbanization of the United States* (Oxford University Press, 1985).

Jimenez, Lillian, *Immigration, Crime, and Neo-Segregation: America's Legacy of Xenophobia: The Curious Origins of Arizona Senate Bill 1070*, 48 Cal. W. L. Rev. 279, 286–7 (2012).

Jolls, Christine and Sunstein, Cass R., *The Law of Implicit Bias*, 94 Calif. L. Rev. 969 (2006).

Jones. James M., *Prejudice and Racism*, 161–3 (McGraw-Hill, 1972, 2nd ed. 1997).

Jost, John T., et al., *The Existence of Implicit Bias Is Beyond a Reasonable Doubt: A Refutation of Ideological and Methodological Objections and Executive Summary of Ten Studies That No Manager Should Ignore*, 29 Res. Organizational Behav. 39 (2009).

Kang, Jerry, *Trojan Horses of Race*, 118 Harv. L. Rev. 1489–593 (2005).

Karasapan, Omer Refugees, Migrants, and the Politics of Fear, *Brookings*, https://www.brookings.edu/blog/future-development/2017/04/12/refugees-migrants-and-the-politics-of-fear/ (last updated Apr. 12, 2017).

Kern, Foxworth, *Marilyn, Aunt Jemima, Uncle Ben, and Rastus: Blacks in Advertising, Yesterday, Today, and Tomorrow* (Praeger Publishers, 1994).

Kimmel, Michael S., *Angry White Men: American Masculinity at the End of an Era* (Bold Type Books, 2013).

Kinder, Donald R. and Sanders, Lynn M., *Divided by Color: Racial Politics and Democratic Ideals*, 92–127 (1996).

Kirk, John A., *The NAACP Campaign for Teachers' Salary Equalization: African American Women Educators and The Early Civil Rights Struggle*, 94(4) J. African Am. History (2009).

Kluger, Richard, *Simple Justice: The History of Brown v. Board of Education and Black America's Struggle for Equality* (Vintage Books, 1975).

Krieger, Linda Hamilton, *The Content of Our Categories: A Cognitive Bias Approach to Discrimination and Equal Employment Opportunity*, 47 Stan. L. Rev. 1161 (1995).

Krieger, Linda Hamilton and Fiske, Susan T., *Behavioral, Realism in Employment Discrimination Law: Implicit Bias and Disparate Treatment*, 94 Calif. L. Rev. 997, 1034 (2006).

Lawrence, Charles R. III, *The Id, the Ego, and Equal Protection: Reckoning with Unconscious Racism*, 39 Stan L. Rev. 317, 323 (1987).

Lee, Audrey J., *Note, Unconscious Bias Theory in Employment Discrimination Litigation*, 40 Harv. C.R.-C.L. L. Rev. 481 (2005).

Lemann, Nicholas, *The Promised Land: The Great Migration and How It Changed America* (Vintage Books, 1991).

Lemons Stanley J., *Black Stereotypes as Reflected in Popular Culture, 1880–1920*, 29(1) Am. Quarterly 102–16 (1977).

Life and Complete Works of Horace Mann (2 vols., Cambridge, 1869).

Loewen, James, *Sundown Towns: A Hidden Dimension of American Racism* (Touchstone, 2006).

Ma, Laurel, *The Real and Imaginary Harem: Assessing Delacroix's Women of Algiersas an Imperialist Apparatus*, 19(1) Penn Hist. Rev. 9–18 (2011).

Marcus, George E. and Mackuen, Michael B., *Anxiety, Enthusiasm, and the Vote: The Emotional Underpinnings of Learning and Involvement During Presidential Campaigns*, 87 Am. Pol. Sci. Rev. 672, 673–4 (1993).
Margold, Nathan R., *Preliminary Report to the Joint Committee Supervising the Expenditure of the 1930 Appropriation by the AmeriFund for Public Service* (1931). Typescript. Page 2 - Page 3 - Page 4 - Page 5 - Page 6 - Page 7 - Page 8. NAACP Records, Manuscript Division, Library of Congress (070.00.00) Courtesy of the NAACP Library of Congress NAACP: A Century in the Fight for Freedom: The Great Depressio.
Massey, Douglas S. and Denton, Nancy, *American Apartheid: Segregation and the Making of the Underclass* (Harvard University Press, 1993).
Massey, Douglas S., Albright, Len, Casciano, Rebecca, and Derickson, Elizabeth, *Climbing Mount Laurel: The Struggle for Affordable Housing and Social Mobility in an American Suburb* (Princeton University Press, 2013).
Mayer, Jeremy D., *Rides the Backlash to Victory: Racial Politics in the 1968 Presidential Campaign*, 64 Historian 351 (2002).
McLaurin v. Oklahoma State Regents, 339 US 637 (1950).
McNeil, Genna Rae, *Groundwork: Charles Hamilton Houston and the Struggle for Civil Rights* (University of Pennsylvania, 1983).
Memmi, Albert, *The Colonizer and the Colonized* (Beacon Press, 1957).
Mendelberg, Tali, *The Race Card: Campaign Strategy, Implicit Messages, and the Norm of Equality* (Princeton University Press, 2001).
Milliken v. Bradley, 418 US 717 (1974).
Missouri ex rel. Gaines v. Canada, 305 US 337 (1938).
Missouri v. Jenkins, 491 US 274 (1989).
Morris, Adalaide, *Dick, Jane, and American Literature: Fighting with Canons*, 47(5) College English 467–81 (1985). doi:10.2307/376878.
Morris, Edward W., *"Ladies" or "Loudies"? Perceptions and Experiences of Black Girls in Classrooms*, 38 Youth & Soc'Y 490 (2007).
Morton, Samuel George, *Crania Americana* (public domain, 1839).
Muddle, Cass and Kaltwasser, Cristobal Rovira, *The Far Right Today, Populism: A Very Short Introduction* (Oxford University Press, 2017).
Murray v Pierson , 169 Md. 478, 182 A. 590 (1936).
Myrdal, Gunnar, *An American Dilemma: The Negro Problem and Modern Democracy* (1944).
NAACP, explained/civil-rights-leaders/charles-hamilton-houston.
Nettles, Michael T., and Perla, Lara W., *The Frederick D Patterson Research Institute of College Fund/United Negro College Fund*. The African American education Databook volume II preschool through high school education.

Oliver, Melvin L. and Shapiro, Thomas M., *Black Wealth/White Wealth: A New Perspective on Racial Inequality* (1997).

Olmsted, Matthew, *Are Things Falling Apart? Rethinking the Purpose and Function of International Law*, 27 Loy. L.A. Int'l & Comp. L. Rev. 401, 423 (2005).

O'Reilly, J., Nathanael Imagined America: Walt Whitman's Nationalism in the First Edition of Leaves of Grass, *IJAS Online*, June 29. 2009.

Orlofsky, M. I., Civil Rights Act of 1875, *Encyclopedia Britannica*, Feb. 23, 2024. https://www.britannica.com/topic/Civil-Rights-Act-United-States-1875.

Page, Antony, 85 B.U. L. Rev. (2005).

Page, Helán E., *"Black Male" Imagery and Media Containment of African American Men*, 99(1) Am. Anthropol. 99–111 (1997).

Patler, Nicholas, *Jim Crow and the Wilson Administration: Protesting Federal Segregation in the Early Twentieth Century* (University Press of Colorado, 2004).

Patterson, James T., *Brown v. Board of Education: A Civil Rights Milestone and Its Troubled Legacy* (Oxford University Press, 2001).

Peabody, Sue and Stovall, Tyler (eds.), *The Color of Liberty: Histories of Race in France* (Duke University Press, 2003).

Pelinka, Anton, *The Haider Phenomenon in Austria: Examining the FPO in European Context, Fall 2001*, 9(1) J. Int'l Inst. (2009). https://quod.lib.umich.edu/j/jii/4750978.0009.10.

Peltre, Christine, *Orientalism in Art* (2005).

Plessy v. Ferguson, 163 U S 537 (1896),

Pomerantz, Gary, *Where Peachtree Meets Sweet Auburn: A Saga of Race and Family* (Penguin Books, 1997; Reprint edition).

Porterfield, Todd, *The Allure of Empire: Art in the Service of French Imperialism 1798–1836*, 132–3 (Princeton University Press, 1998).

Post-War Reconstruction and Development in the Golden Age of Capitalism (2017), https://www.un.org/development/desa/dpad/wp-content/uploads/sites/45/WESS_2017_ch2.pdf.

Potts, Randolph G., *The Social Construction and Social Marketing of the "Dangerous Black Man,"* 2 J. Afr. Am. Men 4 (1997).

Power, Garrett, *Apartheid Baltimore Style: The Residential Segregation Ordinances of 1910–1913*, 42 Md. L. Rev. 289 (1983).

Price, Alfred D., *Urban Renewal: The Case of Buffalo, N.Y.* 19(3–4) Rev. Black Political Eco. 125–59 (1991). doi:10.1007/BF02895341.

Pritchett, Wendell E., *The Public Menace of Blight: Urban Renewal and the Private Uses of Eminent Domain*, 21 Yale L. & Pol'y Rev. 1 (2003).

Randle, Aaron, *America's Only Successful Coup d'Etat Overthrew a Biracial Government in 1898*. history.com/news/wilmington-massacre-1898-coup.

Rather Swamped, *Margret Thatcher Foundation*, https://www.margaretthatcher.org/document/10348.

Rawn, James, *Root And Branch: Charles Hamilton Houston, Thurgood Marshall, and the Struggle to End Segregation* (Bloomsbury, 2010).

Raymond Understanding the Antecedents of the "School to Jail" Link: The Relationship Between Race and School Discipline, 101 J. Crim. L. & Criminol. 633, 636–7 (2011).

Roda, Allison, *Inequality in Gifted and Talented Programs, Parental Choices about Status, School Opportunity, and Second-Generation Segregation* (Palgrave Macmillan, 2015).

Rome, Dennis, *Black Demons: The Media's Depiction of the African American Male Criminal Stereotype* (2004).

Rothstein, Richard, *The Color of Law: A Forgotten History of How Our Government Segregated America* (Liverwright Publishing Corporation, 2017).

Ruechel, Frank, *New Deal Public Housing, Urban Poverty, and Jim Crow: Techwood and University Homes in Atlanta*, 81(4) GHQ 915–37 (1997). http://www.jstor.org/stable/40550189.

Said, Edward W., *Culture and Imperialism* (Vintage Books, 1994).

Said, Eward W., *Orientalism* (Vintage Books, 1979).

Schuman. Howard, et al., *Racial Attitudes in America: Trends and Interpretations*, 99–195 (rev. ed., Harvard University Press, 1997).

Schwartzburg, Rosa, The 'White Replacement Theory' Motivates Alt-Right Killers the World over, *The Guardian*, https://www.theguardian.com/commentisfree/2019/aug/05/great-replacement-theory-alt-right-killers-el-paso.

Scott, Joan Wallach, *The Politics of the Veil* (Princeton University Press, 2007).

Sigelman, Lee and Touch, Steven A., *Metastereotypes: Blacks' Perceptions of Whites' Stereotypes of Blacks*, 61 Publ. Opin. Q. 87–101 (1996).

Simson, David Exclusion, *Punishment, Racism and Our Schools: A Critical Race Theory Perspective on School Discipline*, 61 UCLA L. Rev. 506, 547 (2014).

Sipuel v. Board of Regents of the University of Oklahoma, 332 US 631 (1948).

Southern Manifesto, https://d1lexza0zk46za.cloudfront.net/history/am-docs/southern-manifesto.pdf.

Springfield Race Riot, www.britannica.com/event/Springfield-Race-Riot; https://naacp.org/about/our-history.

Staats, Cheryl, *Kirwan Institute for the Study of Race and Ethnicity, Implicit Racial Bias and School Discipline Disparities: Exploring the Connection* 8,9 (Kirwan

Institute Special Report, 2014), https://kirwaninstitute.osu.edu/sites/default/files/documents/ki-ib-argument-piece03.pdf.

Stanford Encyclopedia of Philosophy, John Dewey, https://www.cambridge.org/core/books/abs/cambridge-guide-to-african-american-history/hamptontuskegee-idea/155FA726E97D8D697CAF37CD69A95EEE.

STOPPING ALL IMMIGRATION: At the Core of British National Party Policy Is the Belief that Immigration into Britain Is a Destructive Agenda and Must Be Stopped, *BNP*, https://bnp.org.uk/policies/immigration/.

Suddath, Claire A., *Brief History of The Middle Class*, Feb. http://content.time.com/time/nation/article/0,8599,1882147,00.html.

Sullivan, Patricia, *Lift Every Voice The NAACP and the Making of the Civil Rights Movement* (New Press, 2009).

Sweatt v. Painter, 339 US 629 (1950).

Teaford, Jon C., *Urban Renewal and Its Aftermath, Housing Policy Debate*, 11(2), 443–65 (2000), doi: 10.1080/10511482.2000.9521373.

Tonry, Michael, *The Social, Psychological, and Political Causes of Racial Disparities in the American Criminal Justice System*, 39 Crime & Just. 273, 300–8 (2010).

Tushnet, Mark V., *The NAACP's Legal Strategy against Segregated Education, 1925-1950* (University of North Carolina Press, 1987).

Valentino, Nicholas A. and Sears, David O., *Old Times There Are Not Forgotten: Race and Partisan Realignment in the Contemporary South*, 49 Am. J. Pol. Sci. 672, 674 (2005).

Waldman, Paul, *The American Prospect* (Aug. 10, 2012), http://prospect.org/article/truth-about-welfare.

Ware, Leland, *A Century of Segregation: Race, Class, and Disadvantage* (Lexington Books, 2018).

Ware, Leland, *Deliberate Speed: Implementing Brown's Ambiguous Mandate*, 22 Del. Law. 26 (2004).

Ware, Leland, *Invisible Walls: An Examination of the Legal Strategy of the Restrictive Covenant Cases*, 67 Wash. U. L.Q. 737, 738 (1989).

Ware, Leland and Davis, Theodore, *Ordinary People in an Extraordinary Time: The Black Middle-Class in the Age of Obama*, 55 How. L.J. 533 (2012).

Ware. Leland and Wilson, Divid, *Jim Crow on the 'Down Low,' Subtle Racial Appeals in Presidential Campaign*, 24 St. John's J. Legal Commentary. 299 (2009).

Ware, Melva, *The Racial Balance Standard is an Inadequate Approach to Achieving Racial Equality in Schools,* 18 St. Louis U. Pub. L. Rev. 465 (1999).

Weaver, Robert, *The Negro Ghetto*, 72 (1948). Originally in Federal Housing Administration, 1939. "Underwriting Manual." Sections 932 and 935.

Welch, Kelly, *Black Criminal Stereotypes and Racial Profiling*, 23 J. Contemp. Crim. Jus. 276, 278 (2007).

Westen, Drew, *The Political Brain: The Role of Emotion in Deciding the Fate of the Nation,* 219–48 (PublicAffairs, 2008).

Wiles, Ellen, *Headscarves, Human Rights, and Harmonious Multicultural Society Implications of the French Ban for Interpretations of Equality*, 41 Law & Soc'y Rev. 699 (2007).

Wilders, Geert, *Marked for Death: Islam's War Against the West and Me* (Regnery Publishing, 2012).

Wilkerson, Isabel, *The Warmth of Other Suns: The Epic Story of America's Great Migration* (2010).

Williams, Juan, *Thurgood Marshall: American Revolutionary* (Three Rivers Press, 1998)

Wodak, Ruth, *The Politics of Fear: What Right-Wing Populist Discourses Mean* (SAGE Publications Ltd, 2015).

United States v.Cruikshank, US. 542 (1875).

United States v. Reese, 92 US. 214 (1876).

Yellin, Eric S., *Racism in the Nation's Service: Government Workers and the Color Line in Woodrow Wilson's America* (The University of North Carolina Press, 2013).

Zecchino, David, *Myth of the Welfare Queen,* 64–5 (Scribner, 1997).

Index

About the Author

Leland Ware was the Louis L. Redding Professor and Chair for the Study of Law and Public Policy at the University of Delaware from 2000 to 2023. Before that appointment, he was a professor at St. Louis University School of Law from 1987 to 2000. He was a visiting professor at Boston College Law School in 1992 and at Ruhr University in Bochum, Germany, in 1997. Professor Ware was University Counsel at Howard University from 1984 to 1987. For the five years prior to his position at Howard, he was a Trial Attorney with the US Department of Justice, Civil Division, in Washington, D.C. He had previously practiced with a private firm in Atlanta, Georgia, and with the US Department of Health, Education and Welfare.

Professor Ware's research focuses on various aspects of civil rights law. He has authored more than 100 publications consisting of books, academic journal articles, book chapters, essays, book reviews, editorials, and other publications in academic journals and other publications. Professor Ware has organized several academic symposia, professional programs, and hosted many distinguished lectures.

Professor Ware is a coauthor, with Robert Cottrol and Raymond Diamond, of *Brown v. Board of Education: Caste, Culture and the Constitution* (2003). He is the editor of *Choosing Equality: Essays and Narratives on the Desegregation Experience* (coedited with Robert L. Hayman with a foreword by Vice President Joe Biden [Penn State Press, 2009]). His most recent book, *A Century of Segregation: Race, Class, and Disadvantage*, was published in 2018. He has lectured and made other presentations to numerous audiences in the United States, Europe, and Africa. Professor Ware is a graduate of Fisk University and Boston College Law School.

www.ingramcontent.com/pod-product-compliance
Ingram Content Group UK Ltd.
Pitfield, Milton Keynes, MK11 3LW, UK
UKHW020208290926
15470UKWH00001B/69

9 781666 961874